AWAKENING
to the
POWER OF SOURCE

YOUR GUIDE TO
CO-CREATING WITH THE DIVINE

JO ANN LEVITT

"Thirty years ago channeling was an occult science not widely known or appreciated. Today, there is growing evidence and understanding about channeling and how we can use it in our daily lives. Each voice that educates and inspires people to tap into their own wisdom about channeling is needed. We welcome Jo Ann's work with its efforts to bring lightness and joy into the work of spiritual channeling."

—Dr. Helané Wahbeh, ND, MCR, Director of Research at the Institute of Noetic Sciences

Thoth portrait used courtesy of publicdomainq.net.

SCRIBES OF LIGHT
P R E S S

An Imprint for GracePoint Publishing (www.GracePointPublishing.com)

GracePoint Matrix, LLC
322 N Tejon St. #207
Colorado Springs CO 80903
www.GracePointMatrix.com
Email: Admin@GracePointMatrix.com
SAN # 991-6032

ISBN-13: (Paperback) – 978-1-951694-72-2
eISBN: (eBook) - 978-1-951694-71-5

Books may be purchased for educational, business, or sales promotional use.
For bulk order requests and price schedule contact:
Orders@GracePointPublishing.com

For more great books, please visit Scribes of Light Press online at:
https://gracepointpublishing.com/product-category/books-cards/
gracepointpublishing.com/product-category/scribes-of-light-press/

Contents

INTRODUCTION

More than one hundred and fifty years ago, Lewis Carroll captured the hearts of children everywhere with his enchanting story of *Alice in Wonderland*. As far as its origins are concerned, it was written to entertain ten-year-old Alice Liddell, her sister, and other members of her family during an afternoon tea party they were enjoying by the river; however, it has since reached families of every stripe and in every direction, across the globe. That's because it has themes which children easily relate to, as do their parents.

"Which way to go?" we wonder. Then we remember that large caterpillar with his hookah pointing his arms in both directions. Although the Queen told the knaves to paint the white roses red in the garden, she might yell at them any time: "Off with their heads." And there's something endearing about a blonde-headed little girl who drank or ate something she was warned not to drink or eat, who then expanded in size to such a degree that her head stuck out of the chimney and her arms were flailing out of the second-floor windows of the house. Like her, you may not always know where you fit in or alternately you may feel as if you've landed in a world you don't recognize. Invariably questions arise as to one's true identity, and we love to play with those ideas—and help you observe that the world you're in actually has a much bigger playing field than you ever imagined.

You may be wondering why this narrative of *Co-Creating with the Divine*, starts out in the middle of a children's storybook. That's what we Guides have called forth in working with Jo Ann, our "author" and scribe. As Light Beings in Light, we have a different take on things. And although we don't always agree among ourselves, even as multiple *authors* of this work—still, we have fun and we're cordially inviting you to come join us down the *rabbit hole* and have fun as well.

Since we tend to draw on a vast mix of stories, scriptures, and recollections as we traverse the Universe to bring you our message, you can probably extrapolate from this that not all of us are Earth dwellers. In fact we're mainly "off-planet." That's why we love *Alice in Wonderland* so much; she's wandering around in brand new territory, trying to decipher events and find her place in it all. Just who are these strange creatures that surround her—these rabbits with pocket watches, these grinning Cheshire cats, or Mad Hatters serving tea? In some ways, we're *strange creatures* as well—like the rats, walruses, and caterpillars running around in that story. We too talk out of turn or do unexpected things. We love to turn history upside down or revise the "script" everyone's reading. We frequently challenge conventional views. And we're excited about the New Paradigm of consciousness that's here with us now.

As Light Beings in Light, we're aspects of the Divine, and we're also on equal footing with you, eager to reveal the secrets of how to find your way into grander, faster, and more exciting creative ventures. Whether or not you jump down the *rabbit hole*, we'd still like to offer you pointers about the nature of Co-Creation and what it means to Co-Create along with the Divine. We would, however, encourage you not to take that next bite of food or that next drink, if it's being offered. For, like Alice, you might grow too large to fit in your *house*, and we don't want to get you into that kind of trouble.

Part One:

Summoning Your Divine Creation

CO-CREATING WITH THE DIVINE: AN OVERVIEW

And so we begin with this first thought: what is all this fuss and bother about the Divine? Calling on the Divine? Channeling the Divine? Imagining the Divine? All of a sudden, everyone's rushing out to find their favorite medium or mentor, psychic or channel, while at the same time there's an appalling drop in attendance in churches, mosques, or synagogues. Some things are being called out now that have not been very high profile before.

But we hear you. We see you. As members of the so-called "Community of the Divine," we have observed this continual development of folks scurrying in new directions while withdrawing from the traditional sources of spiritual connection. Please don't hold us responsible. We are simply Light Beings in Light, tracking, responding, cooperating, and commiserating with those of you who're Light Beings in physical form. Yet somewhere—somehow you got a taste of the Divine. Something lit you up, either accidentally or on purpose, and now your heart is on fire. It might have been a great loss, or a great new find (a wonderful partner, a new direction), or even that Mindfulness Meditation class you took while at home during the pandemic. Or you tasted some newfound freedom out on the ski slope or in the woods—or when your firstborn popped out of the *oven*. What you really got a taste of was of *us*—and of *you*—in the trappings of your most Divine nature. And that led to your unequivocal participation with the Divine through our Eternal Union.

We love the sound of those words, *Eternal Union*. If you consider how unions on earth are ideally set up to support the needs and rights of workers, then consider that our *union* in spirit is designed to support the needs and rights of All Beings collectively—whether in or out of bodies and from here to Eternity. Hurray!

What you are receiving here are encoded messages brought to you by our scribe (or writer), Jo Ann. She is the embodiment of what this text is about; in fact, she is in Co-Creation with the Divine. But she's not different from anyone you know. She may be getting on in years—we won't give you the full count—and admits to faulty memory and quite a bit of fuzz in her brain—but most days her sense of humor is in working order, and she enjoys making fun of everything, including those of us channeling to her.

Recently, when she saw a depiction of me, Thoth, with a human body crowned with the head of an ibis, she couldn't help but wonder if that meant I was working with only a birdbrain. However, I assured her that the picture was merely symbolic; there's no way to adequately capture a Divine being in human form, and if she must know, I am the aspect of Divinity responsible for collating, curating, and storing all knowledge from the universe and from all sentient beings across the Galaxy.

We call these *Akashic Records*, and you and everyone you know will find your collective thoughts and deeds stored within them—in a broad tree-like forest out in the Akasha. These Records are born from *Akasha* itself—the very fine airless ether which is the energetic environment housing all Beings of Light and reflections and remembrances of Beings of Light. When you make a decision to drop your earthly body, you too will join us in the Great Akasha, which unfortunately has never contained a bearded old white man sitting on a cloud. But you will join with us as an official Light Being in Light.

You have this energy running through your veins. You can return to your essence, which is light-filled and connect with Divinity anytime you choose, for that is who you are. But you must understand that although you are no different from us, still you live and breathe and eat and poop and make babies. We no longer do any of those things, having long ago shed our bodies (if indeed we chose to walk the earthly path at all).

We know some folks are averse to the idea of "talking with Spirits." We've heard miscellaneous comments through the years; even Jo Ann has had people doubting her process. "How can you talk to dead people?" they ask her. Some even tease her, like her friend Richard, who declared his appreciation for her work while expressing disappointment that she hadn't channeled Babe Ruth!

But we live. In fact, we are more alive and active than you could ever imagine. And consider this—a good third of your life proceeds somewhat unconsciously. At least for many of you, you may think you're "dead to the world" when you're asleep (although you'll discover later on that that's not really true). However, we have no such timelines or divisions. In other words, we're *awake* all the time! And we're engaged. And active. We talk with you, and we talk among ourselves. We know it is hard for earthlings to grasp how we can possibly be conversant without eyes, ears, mouths, or vocal cords, but nevertheless, we manage perfectly well. In fact, our communications are never troubled with loose wires, stubborn Wi-Fi, or any kind of disturbance in worldwide contact. Everything we say and do is transmitted instantaneously—at the speed of light.

We appreciate the joker on earth who described the difference between the speed of light and the speed of sound. Their suggestion was that you might perceive someone approaching you as extremely *bright* until their thoughts catch up with you through the speed of sound. Then you realize what a dumb jerk is standing before you!

We like that analogy. However, you too travel (even without knowing it) at the speed of light. Your thoughts arrive way before your embodiment. It may seem strange to hear us speak constantly using the voice of "we," rather than "I," but that is how life happens when you land fully in spirit. You are both *I* and *we* simultaneously. You retain your unique individual signature energy and the composite features of your consciousness—but blended flawlessly and harmoniously with all the consciousness of Divinity—and with the Light Beings in Light who exist in multiple dimensions and multiple galaxies. We may be close by or far removed from the Earth Star and even the Central Sun. If you've never traveled to Mars, for example, you can still grasp the notion that there is a different kind of *atmosphere* present there than the one that's on Earth. And the one on Earth is clearly set up to allow three-dimensional life to flourish. But if you leave Earth and travel to Jupiter, Saturn, or Mars, you will need extra equipment to breathe and deal with weightlessness.

In much the same way, leaving Earth to join Divinity, you no longer need your earthly space suit or your oxygen tank. You have entered a completely different environment, and we are working hard now with Jo Ann to describe this to her, since obviously she is still earth-bound and sees through three-dimensional eyes. Yet her heart and mind often join us beyond Earth's reality.

If we say you're just a drop in the ocean, you can understand that notion. A drop can live in a glass of water or the teapot or the bathtub or the toilet. By itself it is just a drop. But when it returns to the river on its voyage out to the sea, it joins with trillions of drops just like itself and seems to merge inextricably with them. What may be hard to understand is that even though you merge with all of us *drops* of water, you never lose your individuality and neither do we. That's because of the nature of consciousness, which you think of as finite, housed only within your head. Actually, right in this *now* moment, your consciousness can be felt, known and recognized as truly and only yours—across the Universe. So if it's not really dependent upon or residing within you physically, why think it would disappear just because you've gone and dropped your body?

No, you've been streaming online for centuries. We like the image of videos streaming to your device. Since Jo Ann loved the movie, *The King and I,* she is trying to picture what it would be like to steam that same video from virtually any place on Earth (or even throughout the Galaxy). It can happen easily, so long as she has a network connection and the appropriate device. Well, once you're in spirit, you are automatically hooked up; you have no need for a charger, a plug-in unit or access to Wi-Fi; you are literally submerged and surrounded by a constant streaming medium. And the main device (and the only one you'll ever need) is that same *device* you have now on earth—which is your expanded consciousness!

How nice to know you came in *fully loaded!* How nice to know you'll exit equipped the very same way, and all along you've had the means and the material present within your own wiring to receive and transmit the Divine. You've never left the ocean, Dear Drop of Water. You are with us even now. The question is—are you ready? Do you wish to take on the joy and challenge of Co-Creating with the Divine? It's a good question. And as always—the choice is totally up to you.

CO-CREATING IS A SPECIAL ART FORM

Do you love to sing? Do you sew? Are you an expert baker or basketball player? Perhaps you hold the secret to investing wisely?

Or you heal or minister to people's needs? Or you can teach small children how to create gardens? Whatever you do or want to do, consider for a moment—what is the chief aspect in doing it that brings you *joy*?

Jo Ann gets a thrill out of watching people come together, questioning their old ideas, and making a deeper connection with their own Divinity. Why else would she scribe a work of this nature? As an energy worker, she also loves to help free up energy so that healing takes place naturally and spontaneously. Now give a thought to something you love to do: what constitutes its core satisfaction? Does it please you to move physically? Or help others access greater wealth and abundance? Or learn something critical and important? Or perhaps you love inventing things of service to others? When you achieve greater understanding of what moves you, lights you up, and inspires you into action, then you will have a clearer idea of the propelling energies that have you seeking new creation.

You are wired to create. As we spoke of in the last chapter, you came in fully *equipped* to interact with the Divine. But you may be wondering what's the big deal about Co-Creation? You may be thinking, "I've been doing perfectly well all these years, fending for myself, completing college, managing my career, my family, and my finances. Why must I get all fancied up with Divinity and turn into some kind of magical Harry Potter?" That's a great question.

The only problem is that it's based on a very narrow definition of who you are in the *wholeness* of your Being, and in a very narrow perception of how it is that you actually create. There are lots of seers and speakers now who'll elaborate the Three Steps to creation or the Five Steps or however many steps you'd like to take, but basically, you're already collaborating with Light Beings in Light and have been all along! "Fine," you say. "If I've been doing this all along, why change course right now?" And certainly no one's asking you to *change course*. We're merely reminding you of your powers and capabilities—many of which may still be lying dormant—and offering you the means to step up and create even more consciously and deliberately, so that those same powers you've been drawing upon now turn into *Super Powers*!

Rather than being some kind of *cosmic tutorial,* just consider this a Refresher Course. For whatever you're doing (and we know you've been up to multiple, magnificent works during your lifetime), we simply want to help you discover the nature of that creation and ways to add more spice and magic to it—in fact, how to gain more and do more with less effort and greater satisfaction. That way you learn how to expand and evolve the magnitude of your creation so that more and more it becomes a match to your deepest desires and your sacred work here on Earth.

It's important to gain greater clarity about the nature of evolution itself. While it refers in some ways to physical changes you go through as you adapt to new environments—such as gaining wings or losing fins, or in the case of humans—trending toward walking upright or losing a tail (or even gaining more gray matter to handle complex problems), this is just one application of evolution throughout the universe. Your physical adaptations are a response to your environment, your village, your tribe, and the means of survival. Your mental and emotional adaptations become increasingly more subtle and complex as your living circumstances change.

Think of a newborn human today soon having to grapple with iPhones, texts, or motorized scooters, in contrast to a newborn coming of age in earlier societies where the most important tool was a scythe or a hoe. Complexity draws out more complex inner workings—which in turn travel back outward to create more complex societies. The system feeds and reinforces evolution on all levels. However, it doesn't end there. Despite all your gadgets and devices, you're still evolving in higher planes. You're learning that *travel* has nuances you never imagined possible—even as scientists invent new algorithms that bring them to the cusp of discovering life on other planets; soon the term *aliens* will become anachronistic. Meanwhile, you're beginning to understand what inter-dimensional travel is all about, recognizing it's not unfamiliar. As a Light Being who just happens to be embodied, you also yearn for connection with those Light Beings in Light who point you to your original home and original means of Creation.

You see, in an uncanny way, your Creation is calling you out, and asking for your help to evolve in its power and efficacy—just as in taking that on reflects back and helps you evolve in terms of your own power and efficacy. It is a two-way street. (Actually my Divine colleagues are urging me to upgrade this metaphor). It's not a two-way street; it's a four-lane highway. Nope—it's an eight-lane highway with access to railway, airport, and space station! And it exists on multiple levels and in many different dimensions of reality. In other words, the more energy you've freed up, the more open you are to inspiration and collaboration, the more you move into the greater emphasis of the "co" as in Co-Creation. This too is all part of an ongoing evolutionary process; you and your works are simultaneously evolving in essence and in form.

You will recall that in our last chapter we spoke about the *Akashic Records*. Imagine this now. You've taken a book out of your local library. Its title may simply be called *Akashic Records*. But you happen to be a plumber, so you open up the letter "P," find the plumber page and suddenly the book expands out to provide all information and knowledge ever accumulated around the art of plumbing. Or it could be you searched for "P" as in pottery. Or "P" as in "popover muffin-making." Speaking of "popping," when you open this book, knowledge literally pops out and takes three-dimensional form right in front of your eyes. What you've withdrawn from the library is different from anything you've ever read, providing knowledge that spans across all time, all direction, and all dimensions. Even Google bows in obeisance to the broad sweep and magnitude of the *Akashic Records*.

So now we're asking you to give this further thought. If in connecting with us, you could receive great clarity and inspiration, drawing on accumulated knowledge from all time-space realities, wouldn't that be incentive enough? Most of our Light Being Friends imagine you'd be happy to accept such a challenge on behalf of Co-Creation!

We are here in Spirit to support you and to grow the wealth of knowledge and expertise together as a *collective* venture. We are not here to overpower, out-perform, or overwhelm you. We have been working together as a team in what we refer to as the "Divine Expansion Project" for eons; since knowledge is broad and vast, we need everyone's know-how involved—we need everyone picking up their oar to help us move this boat forward in the vast ocean of consciousness. Again, my Light Being colleagues advise that the word *oar* is vastly outdated, and they would prefer that everyone add in the *engine* of their own expertise. For we are moving forward collectively on this planet and in the vast galaxies out beyond the Central Sun, and no one can stop that action. It is the nature of evolution itself. So consider this our sole act of evangelism. With all you know and all that you are—it is very clear to us that we want you on our team!

THE NOTION OF A SEPARATE SELF

Now most people have a good idea of what it takes to manifest something in 3D. You've been tuning in for a long time to the notion of magnetism—of like attracts like and of "Ask and you shall Receive." So what's offered here is simply an upgrade. And also an acknowledgment of the growing genius and increasing complexity of what you've created thus far on the Earth plane.

There's just a few "t's" we want to cross and a few dots to add to the "i's." In fact, this metaphor is a perfect match to our message: for in truth, rather than "dot" your "i's," somehow we'd like to turn your "i's" into "we's." For far too long, you've been accustomed to creating on your own and feeling if not alone, then at least unaided, or even unsupported. And sometimes you feel even unchallenged in what it is that you're bringing forth. We wish to disabuse you of the notion that you're alone in this.

You are not and have never been alone in your Earth walk and in all your manifestations. There is a prayer from an old Hindu scripture called the *Atma Gita* (Song of the Soul) (1), which we love. A series of dialogues between Krishna, the beloved deity and his dear disciple Uddhava, there is great advice and encouragement about how to live a holy life on Earth and gain access to Divine Wisdom.

For the purpose of our Co-Creation discussion, we've selected one or two verses that are relevant. Towards the beginning, Krishna advises Uddhava that he must give up the idea of a *Separate* Self, if he wishes to know God. Of course, as you're gathering, we consider that a fundamental truth; however, there are some important sequelae not to be overlooked. In addition to that, we'd advise you to give up the idea of just *One Single God*, if you wish to know God, that is. In light of all our talk about oceans and drops of water, it seems tricky. But the greatest pitfall in human understanding seems to be that you've taken that ocean of oneness—of the consciousness connecting us all—to be equivalent to only One manifest God, which creates a severe limitation in terms of Creation. Remember that that *One God* actually strolled through the Garden of Eden in the Old Testament (He must have felt awfully lonely walking through that vast new world of his), but in the New Testament along came our dear friend Yeshua (more commonly known as Jesus) wrapped in the flesh of a baby! That's a tough role to take on—we'd imagine—trying to rule the world from a manger.

Although the Hindus, with all their precious rites and rituals, set up certain distinctions among their deities, Brahma, Vishnu, and Shiva—with each one responsible for different aspects of Creation; nevertheless, the idea that they all flowed from one over-arching consciousness (and NOT one being) though evidenced in their scriptures, was often overlooked. Not so, however, in these words of Krishna:

Awakening to the Power of Source

The Self is the source of the whole Universe
It fashions all forms of its own Consciousness
Though all forms are changing and soon fade away,
The One conscious Self
Is forever the Same.

From the *Atma Gita* (1)

Such beautiful words! They convey with an economy and brevity what we in Spirit wish all might realize while still incarnate. It certainly does require a big leap, though. It means having the willingness and then getting a gentle nudge leading to the true understanding of Consciousness as the *Self* of all—and not limited to one Lofty Being, sage, or saint. But you seem to focus more on the form, overlooking the Essence. If you cast your "God" outside yourself, then it's easy to observe the traits of goodness, purity, and sanctity abiding in that one destination. But then you do yourself a disservice. You sacrifice knowledge of your own true Nature, giving up the potential not only for true Co-Creation with the Divine—but also for recognition of your very Self as Divine!

So once again, we repeat what we said before: You are not and never have been alone in your Earth walk or in any of your lifetimes or physical manifestations. Of course you can dig your elbow into our absent *sides*, saying, "What do you mean? Who's here? Who's next to me in my bed or sitting in front of me at the kitchen table? Of course, there's no one embodied in front of you, but that's a mere fraction of the *innumerable* beings moving in and out of your life. Because we live in such different dimensions of reality, it's easy to ignore us. However, we're always with you. We're all made of light—you must know that by now. And so the main distinction is that we're Light Beings in Light and you're Light Beings in the flesh, or what we call Light Beings Incarnate.

We're sorry that having a physical body has put you at a disadvantage in certain ways, though you voted for, asked for, and chose your physicality every time you emerged! We just wish you'd remember your antecedents better. It's kind of like being born on Earth, growing up among parents, brothers, sisters, aunts, and uncles and then when you're finally out on your own, completely ignoring them and forgetting you ever had a family. (Some few of us Light Beings in Light, hearing about this now seem to be weeping over your forgetfulness... In fact one songwriter among us has changed the words to an old familiar verse and keeps singing, "Do Love, oh Do Love, oh DO remember me, O Lovey..." We've told them to quiet down but they're quite intrigued with this new song making.)

Of course, we're playing with you here. But it is true that when you remember your broader *family* in spirit, then you recognize that you have so much more help and support than you ever could have imagined. Sometimes Jo Ann rails at us, accusing us of neglect—or at least of uncooperativeness in helping her reach her goals. This is particularly true when it comes to money. During the pandemic, she went to work, then was out of work for five months, then was called back to work, and then again furloughed for another four months. Although she was receiving unemployment insurance, at the same time she felt discouraged and unsupported. Because she had lost a great deal of money with prior publication efforts and had watched her savings and retirement funds dwindle, she yelled at the Universe, saying how she felt cheated and uncared for in terms of money. Then she wondered what was *wrong* with her because she had always loved having good amounts of money and being able to spend and gift and donate to worthy causes, with the thought in the back of her mind that "there was always more on the way…"

Though we did not rejoice that she'd lost money, we were also not in the least disturbed about her situation because we knew inherently what a great Creator she is—and has been all along. And we want to say the same thing about you. If you are reading this, we are certain you are a Great Creator Being—although the extent to which you are involved in magnificent acts of Co-Creation may be veiled or obscured from your view. Part of your work, then, has to do with unmasking yourself from yourself—and acknowledging at last what a Miraculous Creator you happen to be. Don't get caught up in the old fantasy that "Only God can create," unless you're willing to put on your God-like cape and pull out your God-like wand and poof—call something new into being.

THE GREAT CREATOR BEING THAT YOU ARE

Jo Ann is just now remembering an old Platter's song that was most likely cut before you were born. Its first line went, "Oh yes, I'm the Great Pretender—pretending that I'm doing well." (2) She liked the magic of the melody but not the substance, so she changed the words as she went along singing, "Oh yes, I'm the Great Creator, remembering that I do so well. My need is such; I create so much! And my Light Being team's here to tell…"

We love the playfulness of her rhyme. And we love the playfulness that helps you step out of your old relationship to who you are and what you're actually capable of. If you revisit the first chapter of the Bible called Genesis, then you'll recall the various words that were said invoking Creation. "In the beginning was the word. In the beginning was light." And there was sound play and dividing the firmaments, and then creating dogs and horses and bumblebees and flowers. So many wonderful things came along in perfect order and harmony. But somehow you keep looking backward. For a moment withdraw your attention from so much biblical obeisance, and if at all possible—stop seeing it as history!

In fact, let go of your old way of viewing your beginnings. What if *everyone* in fact were present during Creation? What if the God in your Bible included ALL of us, and that in fact it happened to be our trial run—our first practice session to see what we could bring forth together. Phew. It was hard enough to separate the water from the land or the land from the sky. But as we became more familiar and got the hang of it, together we came up with amazing creatures—birds, beasts, fish, insects, humans, and much more. You may scoff at the idea that Creation happened in only six days. But what if ALL of US were present and actually made it happen? Six days was nothing at all in terms of what our magic could bring forth.

We love how the process has expanded exponentially since those Creation days. We love how more and more Light Beings got on board. Imagine what fun it might have been wielding earth into mountains or lakes or turning sand into vast deserts! As you got the hang of it through your many Earth lifetimes, you too moved from

her bank account had tapped out in the hundreds, while heading even lower?

This is the great trap and difficulty in terms of Creation. Imagine if in Genesis, "God" looked around and saw an absence of monkeys? There were plenty of lions and tigers, cows, sheep, and horses, but clearly no monkeys! Now envision "God" (even as a bearded old man) sitting on a cloud, weeping: "No monkeys! Oh my goodness, what will we do without monkeys? I'm so ashamed. How could I forget to bring forth monkeys?"

And suddenly the torrential output of "God's" tears caused serious flooding on Earth. Who knows? Perhaps that was the real reason that Noah had to build an Ark… At any rate, you get the point of this silly story. You can sit and moan and cry over the lack of monkeys in your life, feeling as if it's an unbelievable lapse in consciousness on your part or a serious evasion of responsibility. Or conversely, you can get up and dance! You can congratulate yourself instead on the fine work you've done creating cows, horses, sheep, lions, and tigers!

Essentially, that's the message we passed along to Jo Ann. She had fallen into the "no monkeys" gap and the "no monkeys" trap without taking in the amazing creation of abundance in art and teaching and counseling and writing and many new ventures that were already adding to her savings (including a totally unexpected royalty check that turned up in her bank account)!

Feeling true gratitude is not some New Age *woo-woo* event you repeat while fanning incense in front of your nose. It is instead an interior recognition—an interior acceptance—and an interior basking in the amazing and wonderful things that form part of your daily wealth and prosperity. When you let your focus become absorbed in gratitude for the many known and diverse aspects of your Creation, then it's easier to climb out of the "Gap of Lack," eventually looking back and recognizing how swiftly and effortlessly your gratitude disappeared into that gap entirely. Then lo and behold—you get to turn around and celebrate. Get out some bananas, please! Your house is FULL of monkeys!

YOU ARE THE DIVINE AND THE DIVINE IS EVER EXPANDING

What we mean when we say that the Divine is ever expanding—and that includes you and us as well—is that we are ever expanding in consciousness, in awareness, in new ways to do things and see things and carry out undertakings. Everyone expands and so do all your creations. For you this may include more noticing, more recollecting, and more integrating of new knowledge and information into the reservoir of your awareness. Although you may feel at times that the only thing *expanding* in your life is your waistline, we promise you that much, much more is involved!

Now consider traveling to someplace entirely new. Although your Sat Nat or GPS is giving you blow-by-blow descriptions of how to proceed, you're not at all familiar with this territory. If you passed a McDonald's or an Ace Hardware store, you'd find it easier—for some familiar landmark tends to be reassuring. However, if the landmarks instead include tiny brooks, groves of pine trees, and one rock quarry you may have unwittingly passed your target hours ago. Once you find your way to the old ruins of the quarry (where your kids can actually swim, now that it's filled with water), you can get there time and again; for now you instinctively know the way. You know what to look for. You know all the stops and turns.

It's not a perfect metaphor but the thing we like is how you can now proceed with *ease*. Mastery is like that. Once the task seemed unattainable or much too complicated to pursue; now you know it by heart. But what is expanding? It's your ability to connect the dots—to see the connections. What's expanding is your perspective—your capabilities, and your know-how. In short, it's your entire consciousness.

For like us, you are made of light through and through. We tend to repeat this in the course of our discussion, in case you haven't noticed... As you learn, experiment, gain new skills, new views, and ideas, you keep adding little pockets of light to your already growing lighthouse. Of course, you can't fit all that light into your head—your consciousness continues expanding out beyond you. In fact, from our perspective you now occupy much greater space than that of your physical body. (But no, this doesn't increase the width of your dress or trousers.) You simply occupy more ethereal space. Not only that, your ability to travel and meet up in different time zones and dimensions also continues building and expanding. No earthbound existence alone works 24/7. But all that is continuously fueled by a fundamental aspect of life and consciousness that can be summed up by the notion of MORE.

You are always out hunting—you always want more of everything. And we don't just mean more money, as in Jo Ann's case, but more of everything. You want to know more, to see more, to contribute more, to accumulate more, to experience more, to understand more, to give witness to more and more—expanding out in all directions. In order to fulfill in any of these areas, consciousness must automatically expand beyond its pre-conceived borders—reaching out, accessing and drawing in new areas of knowledge, expertise, and connections not yet "lived in" or adapted to before. And so you move from one creation to the next, gradually gaining in complexity and utility and calling in more Light workers to inform your new designs. Thus, your community of helpers expands; your consciousness expands; their consciousness expands, and lo and behold—a whole new way of life develops out of this.

Again, we quote from that treasured scripture, the *Atma Gita*:

> *When you have gained knowledge and wisdom as well,*
> *When you can feel One with the whole universe*
> *When you've found the Self and in Self found delight*
> *Then you will be free, though you still live on earth.*
> *To everyone loving and gentle and kind—*
> *You'll see naught but One,*
> *And in One keep your mind.*

We Light Beings in Light particularly rejoice when out of your continued expansion, you come to the realization that you're one of us, and one *with* us—Divine-to-Divine. Divine partnering with Divine. Light inside, light outside, with the play of Light joyously dancing, drenching, and expanding us all.

WHAT ABOUT NONATTACHMENT?

If we revert back to our earlier formula, we mentioned instilling Joy into your Creation while also experiencing gratitude for the many forms it's taken throughout your life. What tends to get bypassed, however, is the ability to *detach* from your experience and the intensity of what you're hoping to create. Now, we're not talking about detaching from your Creation itself, but rather from the way in which you hold it, call it forward, and imagine that it will arrive and thrive.

In some ways, the experience of nonattachment is a difficult one for humans. That does not mean that it's unattainable—it's just that it requires certain maneuvers in consciousness that are not always easy to attain. That's because you really *want* what you want—no question about it! But when you want something so hard and with such intensity, your wanting becomes a little careless and often quite *sticky*. What's more, your desire has shifted its origin from the broad palette of Unity Consciousness and arrived instead from lack. When you are seriously attached to a particular outcome or a particular item, wanting things only in a certain way, then you're coming from a place that's cemented in not having, which in essence is the experience of Separation Consciousness. In that case from your observation point, you always see things as separate from you. We like the idea of using the word *blind* to describe that position. You're up in that tree or that self-made *blind* you created. You can see the target but you're also blind in a certain way. And often that means that you're accompanied by feelings of being tossed out or neglected by the great abundance and well-being of the Universe.

Consider this deeply. What is it that you're attached to having right now? We define *attached* as distinct from simply wanting. While wanting something and expecting it to come down the pike any minute, there's a certain ease and relaxation in that wanting. However, when you are impatient or anxious about its arrival or mistrust the benevolence of the Universe (or the state lottery, or the next employer, or meeting up with the love of your life), then clearly there's a lack of relaxation in your wanting. The assumption that it's on its way is now replaced by the fear that you'll never get what you want. So which world are you coming from in this thing you hope to achieve—the world of Separation Consciousness or the world of Unity? It has great impact upon the trajectory of Creation, moving from imagining to desiring to finally seeing it show up on your doorstep.

On the other hand (and we're not totally railing against attachment), it's important to observe how your Creations often arise from this place of Separation. It's really *hard* to be without the love or money or goods or understanding that you feel you require. There is indeed a great deal of suffering that comes out of attachment because you're poised between the wanting and not-having and beginning to blame yourself or others for this unwanted situation. Out of this suffering or not having, however, you begin to devise new approaches. New ideas crop up. New means arise anticipating or even replacing the old *ends*.

Although you may not have entirely succumbed to your *fun* gene you at least are looking for ways to distract yourself from the pain of wanting, or finding new approaches, or inventing entirely new or different activities that fulfill you. So you approach from the *back* door instead of heading in the usual front door way to what you desire. And the so-called back door actually leads you out into an amazing garden replete with new forms, new flowers, new fragrances, and a sense that all is well after all. And as an amazing by-product, coming out of this experience of attachment, you discover that you actually wanted peace of mind more than you wanted *anything* on this planet.

So how to pursue this peace of mind? How to want things in your experience with fervent desire, while at the same time wanting them in a nonattached way? That's what yogis talked about for eons. They definitely had a handle on surrender and nonattachment. We just feel that they took it out too far in declaring that the best thing for a spiritual seeker is *to not want anything at all!* How can that possibly be? It defies reality.

Even if you don't have great schemes for achieving wealth and prosperity, or ending hunger in the world, or saving the climate, still you can't really live and breathe without wanting. Think about it. You wake up in the morning, realizing you're very hungry. So you decide you want some toast and jam. But wait a minute—that's wanting. Isn't that against the rules? (And does that mean you should actually eat something you don't want?) Then you know you really want to go out and take a long walk; however, you realize that since that is contrary to your spiritual practice, instead you remain in bed all day. Okay, we've made our point even though it's silly. But the truth is, not only is it difficult to live without wanting things, it's also pointless. Wants and desires form the engine for your next brilliant Creation. Why would you *not* want to see new things appear?

So we're back to where we started. It's not really a question of wanting versus not wanting. It's a question of the Consciousness from which you unfold your Creation. Coming from Unity means that you're actually living within or in close proximity to what it is that you want. You recognize it as part of yourself, so there's no hurry or worry about retrieving it. Coming from Separation, on the other hand, means that you and the object of your wanting are in separate worlds, removed from one another in such a way that you feel as if never the twain shall meet. With so much of your current scientific community insisting upon evidence-based experience or concrete data to prove that what you want has actually shown up or is on its way, it's doubly hard to wait and watch, or to expect and to be at ease. We could almost sum it up in two short phrases: Unattached wanting = I want it. Yes, it's here now. Attached wanting = I want it, but it will never arrive.

Both of these attributes of course are interacting with your magnetic abilities and creativity all along. If in your work you've managed to invoke the Joyous play and Gratitude we spoke about in earlier chapters, then you're halfway towards manifesting something new. That's because Joyous play and Gratitude are authentic expressions of Unity consciousness. When what you want hasn't yet shown up, however, you can either point yourself toward the frustrations of attachment (which naturally arise because your wanting is so strong) or find ways to reignite Joyous play and Gratitude and get on with it. Whatever your dynamic or mechanism of expression, the obvious leap that's required is invariably moving from Separation into Unity. Sometimes that takes a great deal of time and processing effort; at other times it happens in a New York minute.

TO CLARIFY THE *CO* IN CO-CREATION

By now you may be clear on the nature of Co-Creation. Or you may have lingering questions, such as what *exactly* do we mean by *Co-Creation*? And how might it be different from good ole run-of-the-mill Creation? Of course, the distinction is subtle between the two. Co-Creation involves the essence of creation work, but it's the "Co" that implies the difference. It's a combined effort. It's collaboration. It involves cooperation between you and another party, and in the instance of Co-Creating with the Divine, that's where we step in.

For just a moment, step away from your limited view. Imagine you can fly out the window. Allow your consciousness to slowly drift outward and upward. You now have an expanded view of Earth. Look around at this diverse landscape, and consider carefully. Could this have sprung forth from just one mind—even a very "godly" mind?

As we look out and about, we're suddenly pulled back by the *gravity* of all that's been created on Earth. Right now we're reminiscing about the genius of Henry Ford. Now, of course, we know that his genius did not extend into all human directions; however, he took up the idea of collaboration and organized it into an efficient system, putting complex parts together in exactly the right order to produce cars on an assembly line. Or consider the numerous trials of Thomas Edison. Though such ideas as cars, planes, phones, or electric lights have existed for all time within the Universe, it took a certain kind of genius to go to the next step and pull a working model out of the ether. Why call this Co-Creation? Because in each case, individuals were able to harness new mechanics and new understanding through testing, questioning, revising, and *revisiting* with us in dream time or in meditation. It's not necessary to sit with your eyes closed chanting *Om* in order to access higher dimensions. Deeply focused concentration can evoke the kind of calm and introspection that easily helps you transcend 3D consciousness.

But in sleep, you ask? Do not scoff at this idea; plenty of action goes on during your sleep time; you're not just lying inert on your bed. Of course, you are replenishing your physical body as an enhanced vehicle of consciousness, storing old memories, detoxing your liver, and on and on. However, in your deepest states you are also meeting up with your own privately appointed "Council" to help you actualize your dreams and goals. This may require a brief leap of faith to understand, since few retain conscious awareness of what transpired at night once you're again "awake." But often your listening takes you much deeper into the core of the issue, once you've quieted everything down.

In her years of teaching both at Kripalu Center and at Canyon Ranch in Lenox, Jo Ann trained herself to listen beyond her own private thoughts to hear the underlying narrative of clients or guests. She remembers during one of her lectures on Loving-kindness practice that a woman voiced her resistance about being able to feel compassion toward those she considered "evil." For a moment there was silence in the room. In that brief span, Jo Ann could feel and perceive the woman's tortured heart beneath her stubbornness. With just a few words of calm, she was able to somehow embody the very compassion (which at first was more like a concept than real experience), for that person whose heart immediately seemed to melt, having been received so deeply. And out came tears of relief.

Jo Ann also remembers sitting with a small group on retreat in southern France, listening to a young woman pour out her heart about the guilt and pain she felt in relation to her mother. Immediately sensing the underlying dynamic, Jo Ann asked her a simple question: Are you responsible for your mother's pain? Somehow, that hit a nerve and helped release a long-held illusion for the woman. Again, tears of relief followed.

Now you may be thinking: Yippee-ah-yay for Jo Ann, but what's so great about that? Why do you insist that it's some kind of Co-Creation? And the answer is simply this: When you learn to listen deeply, when you learn to set aside your own view of things, when you put yourself in a position to receive more broadly and more deeply—you've then allowed information and help to pour in from all corners of the Universe. You are a transmitter AND a receiver. But to grasp this with finality, you will need to let go of the notion once and for all that you exist all alone in your world and that no one knows what you're thinking nor do you know what anyone else is thinking. That's simply not so.

Reverting back to our scribe (who provides us so many good examples, even at the risk of embarrassing her), Jo Ann remembers several instances where her thoughts were known to others, even though this was clearly not her preference. While living with the Kripalu community in a small PA town in the late '70s she remembers greatly admiring one of the men who lived there. Gradually her admiration turned into a full-blown crush. He was an extraordinary yogi and at times they both taught workshops together, traveling to NYC and Boston with several other disciples. She remembers once when they were unpacking the trunk of their car, she signaled to him to pick up his bag. Suddenly, he exclaimed with a mischievous smile, "Oh, and all along I thought *you* were trying to *bag* me..." Needless to say, she had a hard time living that one down.

The community was, after all, designed around strict yogic principles of celibacy, disciplined practice, simplicity, and service to others. As she's writing this moment, Jo Ann is smiling because she hasn't touched down into that particular memory for more than forty years! Now we're not trying to air her dirty laundry, but you must realize that in "those days" such strict discipline didn't always extend to the nature of one's thoughts. The following is another example of how thoughts freely circulate and can be known to anyone who has the consciousness available to *catch* them.

Again, Jo Ann finds herself seated in meditation in that small town setting with twenty or thirty others also present; the "sisters" arrayed in their white saris seated on one side of the meditation room and "brothers" in their white kurtas and pants on the other. As she looks around the room, she senses the extreme quiet, in great contrast to the jumbled thoughts in her mind. From her vantage point, she can see everyone with their eyes closed. Gazing forward, she sees the swami sitting cross-legged on the dais directly in front of her, while Bapuji, (3) the revered teacher visiting from India, sits on the right, closing his harmonium after leading a chant. Though everyone else seems preternaturally quiet and self-contained, Jo Ann feels distracted and out of place. Slowly, she turns to focus on the swami dressed in orange, who's just come from India to serve

Bapuji personally. Suddenly, the thought occurs to her, "I wonder what it would be like to sleep with a swami?"

In that exact instant, Bapuji opens his eyes and gazes directly at her. With a big smile on his face, he points his index finger to the ceiling, waving it back and forth—as if to say, "No, no, please! Put that thought away." And so she does. But to this day, Jo Ann not only remembers that stunning moment of "getting caught," but also (and more importantly)—the extreme benevolence that accompanied Bapuji's gesture. How wonderful to be caught and not judged!

IS THIS JUST HOCUS-POCUS?

So what is it we're trying to say? Is this just some new version of hocus-pocus we're foisting on you? Are we hell-bent on coming up with instances of mind reading or psychic phenomena? Not at all.

It's just helpful to know that your thoughts, your dreams, and your actions, (those you've completed as well as those you're contemplating) are ubiquitous and well known far beyond your own head. Awareness is unusual in its elasticity and far-reaching communicative power. If you could equate your thoughts with the movement of something neutral—such as electricity—then you have a better idea of what we're speaking. Electricity can go anywhere there's an appropriate conduit. You could have a lamp, a light bulb, or a wire from your house to the telephone pole. You could have the spark that lights your gas heater or turns on the compressor or the floodlight or the generator. It goes through any channel you provide.

While thoughts mimic that same action, let's say they're a little wilier and more unpredictable. Or let's say that the "channels" are much less uniform while being yet more widespread. Again, *Akashic Records* come to mind. They're part of a beautiful extended quantum field, which has enormous access and supreme intelligence and through which everything is taken in, recorded, annotated, and reserved in archives, with never a judgment as to which experience is better (or worse) than another. And so you have this amazing worldwide and universe-wide and galaxy-wide storage area for all things considered: past, present, or future. If you're a sentient being (as we're assuming you are if you're reading this), then you have constant access, like all of us, to what is stored moment to moment.

When you begin to sense the great plurality of life on earth, as well as "off-planet," then this extreme pride and focus on individuality begins to dissipate, and in its place comes the appeal of instant collaboration and support from the Divine, along with a certain curiosity about what it's like to experience *blended* Co-Creation.

As we said earlier, you don't need any particular tools or training manuals; you've come already prepared and fully wired for the experience. All it really takes now is choosing. Are you ready to undertake Co-Creative work in a conscious, deliberate fashion? And if you so choose, you may begin learning about how natural it is—and not only that—you may discover how you yourself have been dipping in and out of Co-Creation at different times in different ways!

Of course, there is magic to all of this. We wouldn't deny the beautiful, smooth, effortless affair that can come through once we're on the same *page*. Jo Ann certainly feels this way about her writing efforts; in the past she did long research, even traveled to India to gather facts and anecdotes about Bapuji in order to bring together an earlier work entitled *Pilgrim of Love*. Though it was in fact a labor of *love*, she would put the emphasis more on the *labor* in that enterprise, whereas now she has the luxury of sitting in meditation and waiting for inspiration to come through. She doesn't have to wait long. And her scribing feels effortless. As long as she has the ability to concentrate deeply, she can write for hours.

What are these words—these sentences? Where do such thoughts come from? That's part of the magic and the mystery. We're communicating through her, but as we said before, it's more than a two-way street. Most likely you've had multiple experiences of Co-Creating on the Earth plane. Now you can wake up to that dynamic and move more deeply into the work—coming away with even greater satisfaction.

THE HOLOGRAM OF CREATION

Although many of you may be Lone Rangers, sitting at home creating PowerPoints, blogs, or podcasts, somewhere in your consciousness there's still the indelible experience of having sat around a boardroom table or a PTA meeting or even attended a Town Hall where you've truly sampled *collective* experience. Though at times it may have seemed like a contest or a competition, on the other hand, bringing folks together and sharing ideas tends to grow the possibilities available and build even more inspired works through the easy arts of collaboration and association.

Jo Ann remembers a fun group assignment she had when she worked with a New England firm of creative consultants visiting ad agencies in Boston and NYC many years ago. They gathered executives along with team players in multiple small groups and gave them brainstorming assignments generally having to do with something odd or "out of the box." Her favorite was working with a group in Boston whose process focused on the question: "What are the ways that you can turn a king-size bed into a powerful weapon for the offense?"

Given only five minutes and dozens of stickies, groups came up with amazing ideas based on shark-fins, pillows filled with acid, beds turned into tanks, torpedoes, flying bombers, and other outrageous weaponry. (Not that any of these were put to use, of course.) It was just an initial ploy to help the ad agencies think differently about their brands. It was also a way to demonstrate the power of collaboration—once you get on that particular creative "train," then momentum builds exponentially. By a process of association, combined with complete joy and unrestrained creative freedom, groups take thought far beyond its usual constraints. And they wind up having fun as well!

In joining with the Divine—with Light Beings in Light, you too enter boundless dimensions of creativity. You have no idea when you start out exactly where you're headed or where you'll wind up in the end, because, you see—this is not a linear process. This is part of a hologram. And excuse our pun, but with a whole lot of contributors jumping on board, it's a "helluva" whole-of-a-gram.

This book you're holding in your hands or reading online is a perfect example of a "hologram." We're not using the word in its literal sense, for that refers to the creation of a 3D image without the use of a camera (but rather with the play of laser beams whose combined light reproduces a virtual image). But more in line with the origins of this word, *holo* refers to one or oneness and *gram,* whose root is *writing* or *message*; then a true hologram can produce the experience of oneness through writing, or what may be thought of as a holistic or unified experience. The *gram* carries with it the entire virtual experience that can be reproduced and brought to life again and again.

What you receive, then, is a direct transmission. You are cast into the experience; you are not looking at it from the outside. These words come through in such a way that they feel as if they're showing up three-dimensionally, such that you can lift this image right off the page. That is the result of true Co-Creation with the Divine.

The message that's being transmitted comes through multiple dimensions at once, and Jo Ann receives and translates it into holographic images. As we said before, she may be receiving the thoughts; however, she's not just a passive blob sitting on a couch. Like us (and like you), she is both a receiver and a transmitter—so when the initial thought drops in, she adds her ideas, and her descriptives and plucks memories from her own vast *Akashic* reservoir that help elucidate different passages. Since we are in this together, the combined work has the imprint of multiple presences and multiple points of view. In effect, it is a living thing.

THE CONSCIOUSNESS WITHIN YOUR WORK

We change direction a bit in this chapter. Transmitted by an amazing intuitive, healer, channel, and teacher, Danielle Rama Hoffman is a leader in the shift into Unity consciousness and has been Jo Ann's mentor and source of Divine inspiration. Although in the following notes, Danielle describes an advanced-level course she offers online, entitled "Ascended Mastery Academy" helping people get their premier body of work out into the world, what she says in that context applies equally to what we've been trying to get across in these pages. With her permission, we are using her transmission in a broader sense to point to the combined effects of Co-Creating with the Divine:

"It's like having a TEAM of the most brilliant creation matchmakers at your disposal, allowing you to constantly and continuously create a direct line of connection to Source, to download, scribe, and create YOUR OPUS LEVEL bodies of work..."

"Your creations, like you and like Source, are dynamic, alive, organic, and constantly evolving. As you partner with Source you create what we speak of as CONSCIOUS content... It is conscious in the sense that your book, program, or business is conscious, with an infinite intelligence, and unique purpose that exists in multi-dimensions. It is conscious as in you have accessed your higher consciousness to create this body of work consciously. This makes for an irresistible combination of energies that simultaneously contribute to your evolution in consciousness, to the "Earth Star" and to others."

"As you partner with Source and as Source to Co-Create a LEGACY-level offering or book, it is encoded and imbued with Source consciousness; it is multidimensional. Each client, reader, and you as well, access a different dimension of what is in the book and each time you go into it again you access even more from it. This is because the signature energy of the client acts like a key to unlock their bespoke book, or their unique experience in a program. One of the biggest reasons to create your Legacy work with Source from our perspective is the personal evolution that it creates for you as the Creator, the leader, and the practitioner."

"For there comes a time in your evolutionary stage where reading 10,000 books by others will not garner as much inner evolution as scribing your own book. And what is even more exciting from our perspective is that because the content (book or program) is CONSCIOUS and alive, it *grows* with you. Each time you offer the program again, even if you offer it 500 times, you continue to grow from it. It continues to feed you and your clients over time. This builds assets for you and your business and shifts you from having creations that you throw out like a paper napkin after one use to going deeper over time with the same body of work so that it feels new each time you tap into it again." (4)

If a scribed book or program is a prime example of Co-Creation, then you can apply the same idea to works from other platforms. We'll speak for a moment about the art of painting, whether with oils, acrylic, or watercolor. Take a small child who's just learning to put paint on paper. It's a fairly messy process—colors wind up looking either spotty, insufficiently filled in or over-blended, so that everything looks brown and murky. And generally people show up as stick figures. But years later, that same child, now fully grown, has gained dexterity with paint application and proficiency in terms of matching the painted image with what she has in her mind.

Thus Co-Creation begins to occur once you have achieved *mastery* in your chosen area or at least a good amount of skillfulness and expertise. A child first learning to play scales on the piano may work on his own (though there are always exceptions), but when as a teenager, he begins composing his first piano sonata and reaches for inspiration—well, there we are!

Still, you may wonder how we show up. We come through dreams, images, songs, memories, imagination, or even through daydreams. We come through your very own connections to the *Akashic Records* we spoke of earlier. In fact, we have more "channels" or means of relaying information than you could ever imagine. That's because we move about in different dimensions and have access to knowledge from all areas, times, and places; in fact, that swift movement is an aspect of our very own "mastery" and contribution to the evolution in consciousness.

Whether in response to our musician's extreme focus or just when he feels "spaced out," we deposit new themes, twists on the melody, or a bright new ending to the sonata. It's not hard for us to offer multiple downloads, you see. We're drawn to the light and inner magnetism of such creations. And in the case of a new painting, since we have no need to sign off on the composition or receive acclaim by placing our names at the bottom of your canvas, we're simply delighted we can be part of yet another Divine Co-Creation.

In fact now that we're thinking of it, we might go on a painting spree and connect with some wonderful known talents as well as some budding artists-to-be. Any creation can turn into a true work of LOVE, as well as a work of art. In fact, you have no idea how many names would have to be added to the thousands of paintings at the Louvre or the Metropolitan Art Museum if the contribution of us Light Beings in Light were truly acknowledged along with the painters who translated our ideas onto canvas!

SOME USEFUL PRACTICES

A. The Art of Toning

Think of a musical scale in which the notes proceed from lower to higher, as in "Do re mi" and back down again. Now you too have an inner musical *scale*. But yours is unique to you and may not match the higher or lower reaches of a soprano, for example, or a baritone. (Or even a bass.) But it's where your *music* excels and where your Creation comes forth most vibrantly alive and well. In this first exercise, begin singing that old scale modeled on "Do re mi." Now, take the original "Do" a step lower; now take it even lower. The lower you can go without croaking like a frog, the better. Try maintaining that note out loud. You can sing the actual "Do" or simply hum or create a tone in the same register.

When you have reached the lowest tone you can voice, then you have touched down into the notes that correspond with your energy field, in which your sung "Do" matches the frequency and vibration of your root chakra. That's the energy center feeding your system at the base of your spine. Each subsequent note moving up the scale then feeds the next chakra in turn; so by toning from "Do re mi" all the way up to "Do" again, you have fed and nurtured your entire energy field.

Or you can simply hum. Striking one particular tone, hold it as long as you comfortably can. Then move to another tone. There is something very grounding and familiar hearing your voice from inside your head. It may be the simplest way to access a deepened state of meditation, especially when you don't have time to do a more extended series of breath-work and calming exercises.

B. Breath-work

If, however, you have the time, then go ahead and engage in one of the most ancient practices of Mindfulness—which is focused breathing exercise. Although the yogis in Northern India were the first to systematize the practice of breath-work, termed *pranayama*; there is evidence that in ancient cultures the connection between breath, mind, and emotions was well understood and that certain ritual breathing exercises were carried out in places such as Egypt, China, Babylonia, Arabia, Mesopotamia, and beyond.

Try this simple exercise we like to call "Two-handed Breath." This is a simple way to gauge how deeply you're breathing down into the lung space. Sit in a comfortable upright position. Place your right hand over your heart and your left hand over your abdomen. Then slowly begin lengthening and deepening your breath. After five minutes or so, you should begin to feel greater calm, and your lower hand will have been "exercised" more with the deeper breathing than your upper hand. This can swiftly morph into diaphragmatic breathing or belly breathing, with a similar focus. The whole idea is to slow everything dramatically and by degrees, lengthen the out breath to a greater extent than the in-breath. If you haven't tried deep breathing before, then this will take some practice. Give it sufficient time to show its amazing results.

C. Contemplative Walking

Slow walking can be done anywhere that you like—in the hallway of your apartment building, out in the mall on a rainy day or in the forest when the sun's shining. Obviously, the nicer the weather, the more you want to try it outdoors. Basically, your task is to consciously slow down; you want to shift from walking five miles an hour to two miles an hour to half a block an hour. Although we're being facetious, you'd be surprised how difficult it is for many folks to radically alter their gait and tempo into this slow contemplative range. Walking instead is conceived as a means of getting *somewhere*. In this exercise you have to be content to get hardly anywhere at all, while attuning deeply to your breath, your posture and the feel of the earth under your feet.

It has surprising effects, however. Your thoughts—your focus—your felt-sense all shift entirely, and wherever you are, you feel suddenly at home and very much at peace. If there's a labyrinth anywhere in the vicinity, we strongly recommend trying contemplative walking in such an environment

D. Calling All Guides!

In this preliminary channeling experience, you have an opportunity to make deeper connections and to receive inspired help from the Divine. First, take out paper, pen, iPad, tablet, or whatever you use for taking notes. Sit comfortably and use any method you find helpful to quiet the mind; you can even mix and match practices that work for you.

At a certain moment when you feel that your energies and thoughts are aligned and you experience greater focus, poise, and inner calm, pose a question or concern for which you'd like to begin having some answers. You may speak or write it down, as you like. Now, it's time to play with "Calling all Guides." Taking out electronic notes or a sheet of paper, simply write down "Guide Number One." Then without stressing or trying to figure out a specific response, simply write the first things that come to mind. You could use any of the following to help the Guide's responses pour forth:

--From our perspective, we might offer--

--Here's what we know about this--

--We would also consider--

--This path is likely to be more helpful--

Or whatever first occurs to you. Don't linger too long; write whatever pops into your head without judging, critiquing, or even trying to edit. Then move on and in the next space available, write "Guide Number Two." Carry out the same process as with Guide Number One. We suggest interacting with two to three Guides on your first trial run; after that play with as many as you like. You may discover, to your amazement, that you actually receive distinct and powerful messages, helpful to you in a number of ways.

So now that you've called the Guides—what could it possibly be like? What is different? What do you notice about this experience? Here we've asked our scribe to summarize what it's like for her:

Jo Ann speaks:

Although it takes a while for me to achieve the kind of openness and tranquility that helps me sense your presence, there is a moment when everything seems to stop or slow down. In my mind I feel as if I'm ascending a spiral staircase that keeps going up and around, up and around, and I feel as if I'm moving through higher dimensions. Although I may be the one calling the Guides here, it is actually *I* who am ascending to join *you* in your energetic configuration that somehow brings us together.

This moment is filled with intense closeness and presence. It is almost as if life and breath have come to a complete halt. Although of course I'm still living and breathing, but your presence fills the room with such a sense of spaciousness and quiet that I feel still—extremely still. There's so much quiet that even if cars and trucks pass by down on the street, they seem to exist in another reality. The same thing happens with my thoughts.

Though my mind has a singular feeling of emptiness, at the same time certain thoughts will come and go. I may be briefly reviewing the course I taught last night online, or the way I cooked the steak for dinner, or a conflict I'm having with a neighbor. Things come and go but without a sense of solidity; I can easily escape their force field and return to the greater strong hold of *being* right here—right now—in this place of peace, sitting with my Guides.

Then suddenly there's a sense of submerging into deep, deep absorption, receiving your words, images, and multiple downloads. I enter another space altogether. In fact it feels as if I'm in a strange timeless zone. I no longer sense the movement of time in the same way that I do during ordinary consciousness.

While all this goes on and I feel spellbound, it also seems as if you're *holding* me—but not of course in 3D; still I feel surrounded and touched energetically, as if all your *hands* are touching one another and extending this warmth and magnetic energy to me. "There is great love for you"—you seem to be saying over and over again, which helps me remain in that vibration. There is deep listening, encouragement, and support. It doesn't matter what direction I choose to go in or even if I choose nothing at all. It is clear that my choices don't matter as much as my willingness to remain connected. And so in the midst of this Divine partnership I feel that I am held and loved and that there is warmth and closeness, while at the same time there is also enormous spaciousness and allowing. That is the kind of freedom-within-connection I've longed for all my life, and here it is—active—available—and joyously delivered through this magical Union, allowing any new Co-Creative activity to pour forth that wants to pour forth. Even the *sky* is no limit!

IT IS ONLY THROUGH YOUR CHOICE

Although we've put forth a fairly comprehensive explanation, covering Co-Creation basics, you've only seen the railroad cars and caboose moving down the tracks; what you haven't seen up close, however, is the *engine*. None of this would come into play under any circumstance unless the engine itself was fired up, in good working order, and ready to move. And you, of course, are synonymous with the engine. It is your heart, your passion, your vision, your energy, and above all, your *choice* to be engaged in this work of plurality that provides the engine to get us going. It is you and only you who summon us through your heart's desire to expand the platform, the potential, and the power of your creation. And it is by your clear choice that we are then recruited and engage in this Divine process with you.

We're not saying that formal contracts need to be drawn up or that you need lawyers to check our credentials and make sure our contribution is above board. In fact, we don't wish to imply that Co-Creating with the Divine happens only with us Light Beings in Light, as we have described ourselves. Your Co-Creative process goes on all the time, with Light Beings everywhere, both in and out of bodies. It's in that broad nature of Consciousness—in Krishna's depiction of the *Self* of All that such combinations show up.

However, if it's Light Beings in Light who join in this project and are working with you, you must recognize that it's because we've already met and come to an agreement in higher dimensions. No board meeting happened; no HR manager or committee signed us on. It is helpful, however, to know the key conditions that brought us together:

- We met because of your choice.
- We met because we had something to contribute.
- We met because in your own way you called us forward.
- We met because we could see the benefit of combining knowledge and experience—both ours and yours.
- We met as a result of an energetic match—a clear union based in our combined enthusiasm and commitment to developing the material at hand.
- And finally, if you're at all romantic, then you might like to consider us a *Match made in Heaven*.

TAKE TIME OUT, PLEASE!

Take a moment now to sit back and digest what you've read. Some of it, of course makes sense; some parts are illogical or unimaginable; some parts you can simply toss out the window. But most importantly— if given the opportunity—what would you write about your *own* Creation? Where are you headed? We'd appreciate if you could stop and insert it right here. This chapter is all about your contribution, and we hope you take the time to consider what you've managed to bring forth—exploring more in depth the nature of your expertise and your own areas of mastery. What do you notice in your life experience that tallies with any of the ideas expressed here? And what experiences seem to defy or negate what's been offered?

This is crucial to our overall process, since as we've said many times—we're *all* part of this Co-Creation. You are in connection. You are fully wired up. You have something unique to offer, and from here on in your work has to do with distinguishing and identifying your particular contribution. It's not the same as others' work, even if it bears some resemblance, and that's because you've digested and integrated experience and understanding from many different sources and many different lifetimes. You know some things that no one else has access to or has understood in the same way that you have. You appreciate certain aspects of truth and beauty that no one else has grasped in the same way. You have constructed works in three-dimensional reality that pertain to your own way of knowing and being; no one else could possibly come up with the same constructions—even discounting the *copy cats* who may indeed be out there!

So sit and breathe. Relax and attune to your inner knowing. Let some vision arise out of nowhere. Let some thought coax itself into your awareness. Don't try too hard to be the driving force; allow the magnanimous nature of your consciousness and its broad sweep across time and distance to come up with clues. Allow rich new thoughts and knowledge to arise, seemingly out of nowhere, and yet coming from the depths of your own access to Divine wisdom.

Remember Jo Ann's absurd exercise with ad agencies? After ruminating, they came up with powerful weapons made out of *beds*! The sheer idiocy of it! No one would think along those lines, and yet something creative and unusual popped up from the mere act of imagining. So again sit and breathe and find ways to relax fully. Then attune to the vast reservoir of your inner knowing, and see what's on its way. What new idea about yourself and your creative capacity wants to be reconfigured NOW?

As you focus within your own experience, many thoughts and ideas may surface. You may be moved to try out a new direction or a new experience. On the other hand, *nothing* may come through at all. You may use this as an excuse to judge yourself or feel as if you're not among the "chosen ones." Allow any thoughts of that nature to arise and fall away. It is true that this may not be a time of extravagant new Creation. You may be thinking that ever since the pandemic, you've had no desire to really engage in any *deep* process. You're worn out—or disillusioned. As a matter of fact what you may be encountering is a "time out" or what William Bridges used to call a "neutral zone" in his great work called, *Transitions: Making Sense of Life's Changes.* (5)

We are indebted to Bridges for elaborating something that is so much a part of Co-Creation that it's often glossed over or forgotten altogether. That is the idea of leaving the sown fields fallow. Sitting back. Allowing the energies of whatever you've been up to—to actually subside or to reconfigure.

Your so-called *neutral zone* is a very rich time and place in which to reconfigure your own energy and to re-emerge inspired and refocused in new life. Think of it as winter hibernation (even if it was a very *long* winter…). When no idea emerges or when you have no clear sense of direction or purpose, then the important thing is to do whatever raises energy or strengthens your life force. If as a runner you gave up running for a while, then that would be something to return to. If you feel inclined to meditate, then pick up the practice—and perhaps add a brief writing exercise after its completion. Or take up knitting or woodworking or collecting new recipes.

Carrying out the rituals and routines that help you stay grounded while at the same time building your energy body will be key in helping restore a new sense of purpose. The *neutral zone* has no innate timelines. You can't really predict when it will end; but rather, it's like a buffer zone between what came before and what follows next. The most important thing, however, is to keep the experience of *neutrality* present, knowing that sooner or later you will in fact emerge (refreshed and rejuvenated) from this neutral zone experience!

HAVE A LITTLE *TALK* WITH YOUR ROAD BLOCK

The moment arrives when suddenly new life pours in. The old is on its way out. It's almost as if you can feel the inner sap rising. As you begin stretching out to do more, receive more, and enter into greater productivity and creativity, take a moment to reflect what a beautiful life this is! What do you notice about all the amazing things pouring into your life in this moment? And then consider if there is anything still standing in the way that may conceivably be blocking entrance to all that abundance?

For the moment Jo Ann is remembering her friend's particular issues (whom she'll refer to as Louise). Louise counseled and helped hundreds of people with health issues, compromised immunity, or low energy, and though many flocked to her programs or sought her advice on a one-to-one basis, still Louise rarely seemed thoroughly engaged or fulfilled in her work. Often on a night out for dinner with Jo Ann, she'd complain about her greatest flaw—never having sought a counseling degree or her MSW when she was younger. If only she'd have had the foresight to go to graduate school!

Hearing this from Louise so many times, Jo Ann began studying the effects of this kind of thinking. She understood that in certain ways,

Louise was just a stand-in—or better said, a *mirror*—reflecting back how her view of Self not only got in the way of her creativity, but also and more importantly, tended to block her capacity to fully delight in the fruits of her own Creation. And that this could apply to anyone's process, including Jo Ann's.

This helped Jo Ann question what in her own life was getting in the way of full-blown joy and receptivity. As she pondered deeply, out came a two-fold roadblock that stretched across her mind. (And in her imagination—across the road. She could almost see cars backed up behind it and people on foot trying to cross over in order to get by.)

Her two-fold block amounted to this:

1) I must not have what it takes to bring this wondrous thing forth.

2) No matter what I do, it's never enough.

Although she does in fact have an RN degree, a Master's in Education and certification in the practice of Healing Touch, for her it isn't really a question of degrees. Rather it's tied up with a sense of some internal *lack* within herself that can't seem to be overcome, no matter how hard she tries. However, getting these roadblocks out of the way could be as simple as literally moving them to one side of the *road*, allowing traffic to flow smoothly once again, if you get the gist of this metaphor.

It's not as if we're suggesting that you dwell forever on your perceived shortcomings. On the contrary, if you follow the New Age maxim at all—that *Energy follows thought*—then obviously you want to be headed in the exact opposite direction. However, when you've sincerely applied body, mind, heart, and soul to your works and still seem to fall short of the expected results or returns, then it may be a good time for you to sit down and "have a little talk with your road blocks."

COMPARE AND DESPAIR

And gradually you witness the road blocks moving out of the way, one by one. If you're engaged in a great enterprise, it's often a sign that your energy and consciousness are preparing to expand, having successfully met up with one of these delightful "obstacles." In speaking earlier with Jo Ann, we advised her to continue channeling this work of genius, although along the way she'd certainly met up with self-doubt, questions, and not-so-subtle resistance. Although she prizes our interactions and loves writing down word-for-word what she receives from her dedicated Council of Light, still there were moments when everything seemed unreal. Then a little lapse occurred, she stepped out of communion and wondered if she shouldn't just give it all up. "Why should I be channeling you?" Jo Ann inquired. "After all, you already have a perfect channel in Danielle!"

With that, we were obliged to give her an example. Imagine that you're back teaching in high school like you did years ago in West Philadelphia. Although you're teaching American History, you're aware that other teachers in your school have different specialties—such as art, math, science, French, or English. Now, you wouldn't expect the French teacher to step in and teach your class, would you? Nor would you be prepared to go into the science lab and fill in for the teacher there. Everyone contributes to this great *educational effort*—each with their brand of expertise. So this is your unique contribution; let it stand on its own.

Anna, Grandmother of Yeshua, is trying to get a word in edgewise here. So she pops a few lines into our "chat" box. What's she's saying is this: Basically it is not a question of either/or but a question of both/and, as you've heard many times before. If the Universe is expanding, it's only doing so because more of you are tossing your *two cents* into the pot. And speaking of pots, the soup is generally not that good without onions. But if you happen to be a carrot or a potato, then it's also your turn to hop right in!

Even now, with all that she's understood and with all that she's learned interacting with the Divine, Jo Ann still has this question: "Why me?" When she goes on to consider this material, again comparing herself with her brilliant teacher and mentor, Danielle Rama Hoffman, she thinks to herself, "After all, Danielle has been an immaculate sponsor of you, Thoth, and of the whole Council of Light; she's brought us your teachings in multiple volumes. And after each new work emerges, your message is clearer, more magical, and more magnificent than before. What more is there to add?"

Of course we answer her with the very words she brought forth in a previous chapter: *You know some things that no one else has accessed in quite the same way. And you have your own unique way of expressing them…* In addition, we let her know that if God indeed is plural, as we have been insisting through these chapters, then in fact we need a plurality of voices and interpretations to describe US. There's no end to who we are. And there's no end to you either.

That was in fact the essence of Yeshua's cry in a former volume of Jo Ann's, entitled *The Twenty-First Century Gospel of Jesus Christ.* He was very clear that the emergence of different Gospels did not end with the four that were originally included in the Bible's canon. His desire was to keep updating and upgrading the very notion of *Scripture* itself. How can it be reliant upon one person's interpretation or even four (especially since none of them actually walked with him 2000 years ago in Jerusalem)? And how can it reflect the changing values, ideals, and understanding of Consciousness, which itself has an inborn, automatic self-evolving App that has been installed throughout existence and throughout all time? We may be playing with you a bit on this App business, but it really is built-in and inborn to want to know more and to evolve. Yet, Jo Ann, like everyone else, still has remnants of that old way of thinking, or what we refer to as, "Compare and Despair." She's not like others. And neither are you. And the next question that immediately follows is, "Why would you even want to be the same?"

We are happy to announce the passing of that Old Consciousness and that worn-out Paradigm of better than, worse than—or higher than, lower than. We are eager instead, to welcome this New Paradigm of Equality and Love, for we're all in this together—so please take us up on this. Welcome yourself to the Divine. And welcome the Divine that is equally alive in you and currently kicking up her heels within your own Being.

ASK YOURSELF THESE QUESTIONS

If you've come this far, then it really is time to roll up your sleeves and move into action. You've had time to think about the ins and outs, the ups and downs, and the whys and wherefores of Co-Creating with the Divine. But don't spend time overthinking this. Go back to your prior analysis; what are your outstanding qualities, your points of genius or acquired mastery? Now, begin formulating the next steps that will take you from here to Creation.

Sit for a moment and just let thoughts move in and out in random fashion. You may be struck by a particular word or image; you may decide to write a few lines or draw a picture. Some folks respond best to auditory prompts, so you could also pull out your phone and record some ideas for future reference.

Then consider what is important for you to call into Creation? What are you feeling drawn to do or be? What learning might enhance your abilities or connections at this point in time? And the next question to consider is: what major *contribution* do you wish to make to the world? What is it that's uniquely yours to have and to give to others, which the very giving of then bestows a sense of grace and completion for you in your own life?

If you've begun sketching that idea in your mind, then the next, equally important question to ask yourself is: in what way would you like *help* to make this offering? Where do you need knowledge, ideas, or perspective in order to bring out more of the beauty and value of your own hidden gifts? These are important questions that may take time to fill in completely with substantial ideas; then again, you may have a gut-sense or instant knowing as soon as each question crosses your mind.

Allow this to be a starting point—almost as if you've made your first sketch of the design on a piece of paper; however, the ultimate painting will miraculously come through in full color on your canvas.

A "MEET-UP" WITH SOME GUIDES

Although Jo Ann has a broad Council of Light Beings who guide and speak to her on different occasions, she is most attuned to what she calls her little triumvirate: Yeshua, Thoth, and Anna (the Grandmother of Yeshua). All three of us speak through her, but each of us may come forward in different ways, depending on the topic.

This is Thoth speaking in this moment. I am enclosing a nice painting that Jo Ann found (for free) on the Internet, so you can get a better idea of what I look like. You'll just have to imagine what I sound like, but perhaps you can imagine a friendly uncle or professor or someone giving you good advice (like your local shrink).

This is Thoth

It is a privilege and a delight to be called forth on these pages. All of us are delighted about these communications—and about the new platforms and portals that are developing to give you access to our Divine partnership. If you follow us back to the peculiar version of Genesis written earlier, then you will understand that the one thing we all love and are proficient with in Spirit is the ability to gather together and play! Just play. Of course, it's much easier for us to be "nonattached" to certain outcomes since we have nothing physical with which to attach ourselves. But we draw great joy and fascination with any of your new works unfolding and our efforts always have to do with helping you release your great creativity out into the world while at the same time letting go of arguments, resistance, or the old dinosaur thoughts that have you thinking you're not good enough or worthy enough to make this happen.

It is truly amazing to watch the endless elasticity and universality of knowledge as it expands even farther with each new contribution. And as you contribute your bounty, your bounty bounces back to you and in its magical way contributes to your evolution and expanded knowledge. You may not realize it, but there are lots of *monkeys* in your house!

And now this is Yeshua coming forward to speak, following my dear brother Thoth's introduction. Naturally, I have no formal photo to share with you; however, you'll find as many representations of me out in the world as your heart desires, though in truth, they all look a bit different! Some may look like how you want me to be, or how I used to look, or how artists think I'm best represented if I'm to be up there in the nave of the church. Take your pick! It doesn't really matter since essentially, I am who I am. Those of you who know me recognize me by my signature energy or essential energetic presence. And I'm always happy to be invited into your prayers. I'm equally happy to be called in to participate, along with Thoth and Anna, to support you in your latest venture.

Although you may hear us speaking, you must realize that we're just a few of the millions of Guides available to you. You may want to check out the last book we worked on with Jo Ann to get more information on receiving guidance and how to tune in more easily. It's called *Channeling the Sacred*, and you'll find plenty of different Guides in there. You'll also find many notes, or what you might consider *bread crumbs*—only they're not leading you to the old witch's cottage; rather they're gently leading you into the great forest of *Akasha*, where you'll find everything you need.

I want to embroider a bit around some things Thoth recently discussed with our scribe, Jo Ann. Perhaps you'll remember that poem that Edwin Markham composed a while ago, called "Outwitted":

"He drew a circle that shut me out-

Heretic, rebel, a thing to flout.

But love and I had the wit to win:

We drew a circle and took him in!" (6)

This poem applies to you as well. You can draw a circle and leave yourself out, or step right in and let the circle surround you. What we're driving at is inclusivity versus exclusivity. Needless to say, you can imagine which version is connected with Separation and which is part of Unity Consciousness. We're asking you to please

give up this constant need to exclude yourself from the goodness of the Universe. You are included, Dear Ones. You are wanted. We love you and want you with us—always. Who you are is precious to us.

This may not be an easy thing to imagine or to draw into your experience; however, if you go back to the chapter presenting different exercises, you'll find that any one of them that you choose may in fact help you feel connected, accepted, and back in the warm *embrace* of Spirit. We're always hoping that you return to that. And know that moving from Separation to Unity Consciousness is a perfectly natural part of your earthbound experience.

It also requires you to make a choice. When you're feeling hurt, victimized, or in some way excluded, it takes great will and patience to return to the center of your being and the tender core of your heart where love and only love exists in every moment. It may not be possible to have love restored from someone else. However, it is *always* within your power to fully experience love, once you've tapped into your heart's essence.

Now, it's my turn. This is Anna speaking, and I'm happy to hear from my grandson Yeshua—as well as to have the chance to enlarge on his ideas or even move in a new direction. Sometimes it is difficult to accept that you truly belong—or that you are truly loved, when you may lack evidence in real time. Or at least lack evidence on your terms.

But we're asking you to begin looking for evidence on *our* terms. That means paying less attention to the thoughts that toss you off the tracks or bring up feelings of distress or despair. It's not that they're not real, for they certainly are, in the moment. However, the feelings of not belonging or not being fully loved belong in one small corner of consciousness. It may seem for the moment that the pilot light in your heart has gone out. Yet, when you move into another space, or take deeper breaths, or move out of such a constricted environment, then you arrive into the greater multiplicity of consciousness, and with it the remembrance that you are loved. The pilot light is always on.

In fact, you have reconnected to the Source of your own love. You've accessed Source and have stopped dancing around the periphery. It's not only that you are loved; you *are* Love. It's not that you must ask us permission to join; you give *yourself* permission because you know you're One with all Beings. Welcome to your Divine heritage, Dear Ones. It's not as if you're not welcome here—for you certainly are, but we're hoping you discover that you're *already* here. Hallelujah!

But wait a minute—there's one more Light Being wishing to introduce herself!

Greetings, I am known as the Over-lighting Deva of Money. You may find that charming, strange, or ridiculous. Nevertheless, there are a host of us—in fact, millions—who function as both Source and Overseer of all aspects of Creation. You have your Devas of love and of music and math and beauty and health and art and architecture and commerce and on and on and on. And here I am, the Deva of Money.

Although I arrived in response to Jo Ann's call, we don't need to rehash her story. But I do want to emphasize the importance of gratitude—which we spoke of in great length earlier on. It's easy to get caught up in the unfairness of the world in terms of money—of how this costs too much—how corporations are thieves—how you've been deprived or swindled or cheated or over-taxed or under paid—by (you name it)—your work place, Medicare, the shopping outlet, the auto agency, your insurance premiums, the super-store, the IRS or your favorite online emporium.

Yet all that constitutes a train-to-nowhere. At the same time, we're constantly amazed at how many people hop on that train (and in some cases never get off). They come from far and wide, rich and poor—for riding that train has nothing to do with how much money you actually have. The only *ticket* you seem to need is "Lack." In fact, you have no idea how many millionaires are simply riding the caboose with "Not enough."

So a two-hundred-dollar royalty check in most people's eyes is hardly worth a *shout-out*; however, it is evidence that you've received something worthwhile from the Universe. The question is: Will you scoff at the amount or *actually receive* it? When you receive whatever it is that has come to you—whether puny, large, or extra magnanimous—that very act of receiving and of gratitude serves as the fertilizer that makes your Abundance Garden grow. That same gratitude becomes fresh water streaming from the garden hose. And in addition, it's the very LIGHT of the sun.

CHANGE OF ENVIRONMENTS

So we're slowly arriving at the conclusion of this section. We know you're getting a better idea of Co-Creation. We also sense a question that may still linger: "Is such a thing really possible?" Or the fear that overshadows other thoughts, such as: "Am I really *worthy* to embark on such an enterprise? How can I imagine myself among your *exalted* company?"

Even in moving toward completion of this work, these same thoughts run through Jo Ann's mind. "Why did you Light Beings decide to work with me? What about others who are so much closer or have so much more knowledge?"

Though we rarely choose to focus on questions arising out of Separation consciousness, still we're glad to acknowledge that these same thoughts likely arise in any Co-Creative process with the Divine. You could call them *dinosaurs*—relics of your long-distant past. They are simply evidence of partially awakened or even unconscious consciousness. In truth, they have nothing to do with who you really are or with the fact of who we are in relation to you.

So we draw again upon that idea of comparison. It's not easy to compare items that are totally different from one another. You can take an orange and compare it in size, shape, and color with another orange; that's simple. However, comparing it to a banana has drawbacks; in a sense it's like referring to two different *species*, even though of course, they're both fruit. In an odd kind of way, we too are a different species from you, living totally as Light Beings in Light. Of course this allusion only goes so far; obviously we share the same inherent qualities, since all of us are made of Light—so you could say that like you, we are also *fruit*. But once you drop your body, you have no difficulty remembering your true essence and the greater impact and identity of your total Being.

Still, we sympathize with you on Earth because we recognize that having a physical body and walking on *terra firma*, while it gives you the advantage of practicing your arts in solid form—it does create somewhat of an illusion that that's what life is all about—which then gives way to the concept that there's nothing else to be experienced, either before, after, or in-between lives. What can we say? You surrender one way of knowing and living to immerse completely in an earthborn existence. We're not calling it higher or lower, better or worse. Again, like your imaginary trip to Mars or Jupiter, it simply provides a different *environment* in which you can learn and grow.

And what a beautiful environment you have on Earth! So many different types of land—mountains, deserts, forests, oceans, rock formations, beaches, glaciers, with so many species, languages, people, inventions—ways to communicate—ways to get things done. Take note for just a brief moment of the broad diversity and variety of life on Earth. Because it provides so many different outlets to test your creation skills, we might then refer to it as the "Cradle of Creation." However we'll hold back on using that other epithet: "Cradle of Civilization"—because that tends to relate to places other than Earth—though things are changing. Still, there's a lovely give and take when you advance the quality of life before you. As you produce and amplify the effects of Creation, you grow your own consciousness in the process and everyone benefits from the expanded state of beauty and abundance. It's truly a powerful means of evolving.

So it's understandable that you've returned to Earth for a re-run or a new set of trial experiments, despite the fact that in the past it has been an environment provoking comparison, competition, and a certain quality of questioning or self-doubt. It still serves as a perfect "playground," however, for testing your Creational skills. If you find yourself still beset with questions, then know that you're working from assumptions originating in the Old Paradigm. Like wondering what's wrong because you've worked so hard and still haven't made your millions. Or haven't yet met the love of your life, despite years of searching.

Such questions arise in environments that are more divisive—more focused in individual results rather than group consciousness or in Creation for the good of all. We would give you the example of someone, who for example, amasses an enormous fortune working at a Mega-corporation, while severely underpaying his or her employees. At the same time there are extremely wealthy patrons creating foundations that improve worldwide health or create access to clean resources. Please don't hear this as critique or criticism. It is simply a means to point out the old way of succeeding (which arises from the very nature of duality itself) versus the newer mode based in Unity consciousness. What would you say your starting point is in this moment?

One thing we want to impress upon you, no matter how your thought process turns out is to let go of the old *judgments* about it. They just send you down another kind of *rabbit hole*—and one that's harder to climb out of because of the heaviness with which you're *weighing in.*

Instead rejoice! Be glad! Embrace everything you're doing, for you really can't get it wrong in the greater scheme of things. Remember how many light bulbs Edison turned out (or Westinghouse) before they got it right! If you fully accept this notion of Evolution, is there any reason to believe that you're the one exception to the rule—and the only one who's not going to benefit from a continued expansion in consciousness? As you evolve, you discover that you're naturally drawn to create in ways that not only benefit you but also benefit the good of all. How could it be otherwise, if you truly grasp the nature of reality; the *Self* of one is the Self of all.

And finally, realize that the Earth herself is in the process of transforming—of upgrading her consciousness. Like you, she is moving from duality to the experience of Unity consciousness. That means she and you gradually become drawn into awareness of your connection with all beings—and all aspects of life. Arbitrary separations or divisions fall away. This process of evolution involves all sentient beings and the Earth too is a sentient being. Each has their own role to play and means of learning, growing, and evolving in new directions, and soon the upgrade will be fulfilled in universal terms. From our perspective, then, the Earth will literally be *glowing.*

THE SECRET TO RESTORING ALIGNMENT

As it turns out, restoring alignment seems to be the predominant question of this age. Even without voicing the concern, you seem to be questioning us all the time—How can I remain centered and calm with all the tumultuous goings-on around me? We know you Light Beings in Light preach Oneness, Divinity, Unity Consciousness, and Co-Creation; however, you're *perpetually* in the Light whereas we swing back and forth, and "in and out" the window?

It is a powerful question and at the same time not that difficult to suss out. You already have the ways and means at your disposal; after all, you didn't just sit down to meditate for the first time in your life (with a few exceptions, of course). This isn't the first time you offered prayers of intercession. You didn't just beat the ceremonial drum before starting your vision quest for the first time nor light a candle in front of the Virgin Mary. You have been poking around in Mindfulness states long before our friend Jon Kabat-Zinn coined that particular phrase.

But now, take that question a layer deeper. After exploring the reasons why you might jump out of alignment (and we're actually not encouraging you to make too *deep* a study of this—considering that you've already done so through lifetimes and lifetimes). However, you can probably notice the general themes that pop up or see a thread that runs through that business of separation; it's usually consistent with "I'm not good enough," or "No one loves me," or "What I have to say doesn't matter...."

To restore alignment, the first step is enhanced *awareness*. The more aware you are, the more access you have to choice. There are psychologists who've written volumes on this, all of which can essentially be boiled down to one main idea: "Awareness *itself* is curative." As you begin to see what instigates your movement toward separation, you gain clarity and at the same time, access to a new response. Sometimes you even catch yourself in the act! That is, in the act of making a choice to derail yourself or go out of alignment over something or other (no matter how subtle the maneuver.) In fact, along with awareness is the willingness to take responsibility for that movement; it is only you who separates yourself from Source. No one else can do it for you.

Heightened awareness is key, but it's not all there is to the equation. Once you see the derelict pattern, the next and often most critical step is to observe and allow. We'll say it again, "Observe and allow." Observe and allow. In that action, you give up the need to make yourself or anyone else bad or wrong. You let go of judgments, which would otherwise further exclude you from that exuberant state of Oneness you so desire.

Consider it as a training ground. In the Old Paradigm, you gained incredible mastery in mounting the various reasons why you should *step out of line.* In the New Paradigm you are gaining mastery of a different sort altogether. You are learning to create a broader and vaster *container* than you've ever had before. And it is you who are the container; it is you who are now able to hold and contain so much more.

What do we mean by that? Imagine that you've just had a quarrel with a friend or a sister or a boyfriend. It was quite a breakdown and you not only felt hurt and wounded but also completely misunderstood by that person. In your mind, you weighed different options and decided you might: shun them and avoid all contact—or write off any future get-togethers—or retreat into your own space—or even retaliate in some distinct fashion.

Now in your imagination, take all of those potential reactions, hold out one hand and place them in that hand, just for the sake of this "argument." We're not trying to negate or make them disappear but rather to acknowledge that for the moment these feelings exist and you have a right to feel them.

However, that's not all there is. Hold out your other hand (in your mind's eye), and imagine now that you can gather up all the love and affection you have felt toward this person, despite this current impasse between you. Imagine also that you can hold in that same hand all the love and caring they've had for you. It may be difficult to summon; however, by the very nature of Unity consciousness and the fact that love is at the core of everything—with patience you will be able to conjure love sufficient to place in that other hand.

Of course, this illustration only goes so far. But what we are demonstrating to you is the way in which you can extend your own boundaries—to contain much more than you ever have before. You are greater than this dispute and your Love is much wider, broader, and deeper than you ever imagined. Your Love has no problem containing these *polar opposites* and enfolding them back into Unity and Oneness.

After any kind of difference or even a momentary sense of alienation, this is a good exercise to try out. Jo Ann remembers a friend of hers whose late husband was prone to get riled in heavy traffic, or when driving behind slow, unconscious drivers. If someone who was traveling very slowly refused to get out of the left lane, he would often shout at the top of his lungs, "Get the hell out of the way!" Then he would quickly add the phrase, "God bless you." Blessings canceled anger very effectively.

Even in a situation without conflict, there are often incongruous moments —such as attending a funeral and feeling great grief for your loss, while at that very moment a friend tells you a ridiculous joke. Can you let yourself laugh as well as cry? In another example, can you accept that there might be an instance where you give vent to fierce anger and just as suddenly find it melting down into peace or neutrality? It's important to know that you have much greater bandwidth than you ever thought possible and that you can, in fact, contain these opposites and integrate everything back into Oneness and back into Wholeness.

Through all of this, of course, it's important to continue whatever practice of Mindfulness you may have picked up along the way— anything that has the capacity to bring you back into alignment and that reminds you to live from your essential Oneness. This is a good time to apply all that you've garnered from lifetimes of spiritual endeavor, for you have more resources than you give yourself credit for. Use prayer. Use Nature. Use hiking. Use immersion in water. Use hot springs or cold compresses. Use mantra. Massage. Meditation. Music. Singing. Humming. Silence. And of course, join with us, your Guides, whenever you can. We too provide support, helping you restore the *container* of your own acceptance by accessing that same broader platform that already exists within you as a Light Being incarnate.

BACK TO THE BEGINNING

There's a traditional Hebrew prayer before meals, that translated in the old way might read, "Blessed art Thou, O Lord our God, King of the Universe, who bringest forth bread from the Earth." But we want to play around with it a bit. So now we've changed the words and the translation to read, "Blessed are You, Divine Playmates of Ours, Creators with us of the Universe, who bring forth bread, beauty, and bounty from the Earth. Amen."

Well, at the close of one section before starting with another entirely new one—we find ourselves winding our way back to the beginning. It is a cyclical process—so just like the Earth, we've made our revolutions around the sun, and we're coming round to where we started out. As we mentioned in the beginning, this is not a linear exposition; you might imagine it more like a spiral in which we go round and round, gradually winding our way upward—to achieve a grander and more global view. What can you see from these heights? What new prospects are offered via this enhanced perspective? Hopefully, the means have already come to you to engage with your creations more deeply. And perhaps within that same process comes an emerging sense of your own *ascendancy*—of your own genius and mastery clamoring to be set free.

There is indeed a great sense of freedom, once the principles and mechanics of Co-Creation are grasped. You know that you now have amazing and unstinting support. You know that deep concentration comes naturally. You recognize that you have a contribution to make that's uniquely yours. You know that it's time to bring out the fruits of your own skill and mastery. You also know that wanting is important; so is the power of your choice. And with all that wanting, it will also be important for you to step out of the way, to want via the nonattached version we described earlier in this work. An additional requirement (though not set in stone) is the notion of patience.

If you've put the cake in the oven, you've got to let it go through its full baking process. If you keep opening the oven, then the cake is likely to cave in in the middle. Naturally, it will take the prescribed amount of time to bake that it takes! In the same way, it takes patience to allow your new Creations to unfold. It takes energy, focus, and clear intention to move out of the Old collective unconscious view of yourself as a sub-division among Beings—as separate, unseen, or unknown. When your consciousness evolves and expands, you literally extend out and move beyond the illusory walls of your separate being to remember and revitalize your full connection with Spirit. Then your Brilliant Light is seen and recognized by Light Beings everywhere.

While Jo Ann is writing these words, she is aware of this powerful connection. Hers is a blended consciousness—where she has free access to us and we to her, and there's a continuous exchange of ideas going on, both consciously and unconsciously. She laughs when she remembers the first time that the image of Alice in Wonderland *dropped* into her mind. Even when she was writing that introduction, and images of Alice kept recurring, she had no idea what direction we were headed in. Frequently she might ask herself, "What's next?" and although we invariably respond with new content, it may not necessarily be the way she imagined it. Nevertheless, out of such combined efforts, something emerges which is greater than the sum parts of us all. Not that we can be broken into *parts* anyway.

It's funny how that same image of *parts* brought up an old story from the Bible, when Yeshua went to visit his friends Mary and Martha, relations of dear Lazarus. You will remember the distinction between these two sisters: Martha rushes out to serve him a meal, then washes the dishes, cleans the house and sweeps the floor, while Mary sits obediently at Yeshua's feet, waiting to take in his wisdom teachings. At the critical juncture when Martha begins complaining about her work (and why can't her sister get off her bum and give her a hand), Yeshua makes his strange pronouncement to them both, that by and large, Mary got the better *part*.

So, tongue-in-cheekly we encourage you to leave off so much worrying, scurrying, hassle, and busyness, for now you have the better *part*! For just this once, sit, rest, and receive. Remember that good old breathing pattern? All that's really needed is to slow it down. Temper your breath; temper your thoughts, and watch your heart rhythm slow down. Seriously—so much of what's needed is actually so little—it's just slowing the speed and timing of everything. Conversely, once you slow the works, you find the means to move with perfect speed and attention to detail. And if you must know, you are not competing against one or the other sister in terms of the Biblical story. In truth, both Martha AND Mary are part of you. They just live in different parts of your consciousness.

So leave off all ruminations for now. Leave off thoughts of the future and thoughts of the past. Instead join us where we are—which is always here and now. Join with your own Guides and *Guidesses*, (we love such puns) to discover even more of value as you continue growing and expanding your consciousness. Who knows? There could be a whole new direction to take, a new body of work on its way, a new hobby or vocation just waiting on your doorstep or stepping out of your dreams! Something's invariably moving to the forefront. And everyone is here to remind you that you're an amazing and unique Creator Being.

As you settle in, relaxed and fully expectant in your comfortable surroundings, take a moment and look around. Take in the presence of furniture, carpets, window treatments, art on the walls, or clothing in your closet—all vital parts of your three-dimensional life. Then shifting consciousness, take in the more subtle presence of your past, present, and potential works in progress—everything you've been creating ever since you began your Earth walk. Give thanks, then, for this amazing bounty, knowing even as you do, that more is on its way.

Take a few deep breaths. Now you can sense that something's changing in your environment— when you look up, you'll immediately see what's happening. Creatures are out in big numbers. They're jumping up and down. Surely you can see that your house is full of monkeys!

Part Two:

Further Notes from the Scribes

In the following chapters, Jo Ann unveils information about what has developed in her process of channeling, downloading, and reviewing new materials that have turned up and are appropriate to include in this Guide. For a brief time she thought she had lost the thread altogether. But now after a brief hiatus from writing, she is happy to announce that she's back—and comes with advice from a number of new or totally unexpected Guides. Along with that, she wishes to acknowledge that many of these Guides have emerged from unknown planets or different species altogether.

SUZANNE CHANNELED FOR ME ON MONDAY

There was a moment in time when, as author and scribe, I hit a roadblock. I knew there was more forthcoming; however, I had felt my inspiration beginning to dry up. Although I don't usually panic around slowing down during the writing process, still I needed to use my remaining time carefully because I had been called back to work at Canyon Ranch in the Berkshires, and I had roughly three weeks to complete the work I'd already begun.

So what to do? First, I sat in meditation and summoned the presence of this Guide itself. As Danielle mentioned earlier, channeling Thoth in in an earlier chapter, it's important to recognize that whatever you bring forth has a life of its own—and through your efforts, acquires a distinct and very personalized consciousness. I would say, without hesitation, that this work definitely has a mind of its own and in our conversation, it insisted several times that no more could be added unless it was totally in alignment with the message and tone already present.

So the monkeys are quite active—even now! They seem to be cavorting around my living room at this moment, landing on top of lamps and bookshelves, complaining that there aren't any good branches for them to swing on, enabling them to cross the room back and forth at ceiling height. Smack in the middle of that rather surreal conversation, I received a call from my dear friend in Florida—Dr. Suzanne DeWees, who's a psychic and healer herself. No sooner did I express my writing dilemma to her than she immediately began channeling information spontaneously.

"You need to go back to Noah's Ark," Suzanne stated right in the beginning. "What?" I replied, for this was unexpected. "You have not yet mined all the amazing detail and information you can receive from the animals on this planet," she went on to say. Mentioning an old work that included poems from different creatures (entitled *Prayers from the Ark*) (7), the gist of Suzanne's message was how important it is for us to trust our furry friends. To listen to the dogs and sheep and woodpeckers and baby lambs—since animals are at one with Nature, they give us great incentive to return to our own connection, at the same time recognizing how much we have in common with the animal kingdom. To truly attune to Nature means that we truly attune to our own energy and spiritual connection. She further explained that nothing quite helps us open to Nature like those animals that live always attuned (other than the pure messages we may receive from our own hearts).

Suzanne herself has always been deeply connected to the feline community and could almost be called a "Cat Whisperer," or better yet, a "Cat Rescuer," since she was the key person in her small village to round up and care for the local feral cats. However, she has an affinity to many different species, and my favorite story is one she told me the day of our "Nature" channeling.

Suzanne had gone to Miami with her husband to visit a close relative and one day she was out taking a walk on her own, enjoying the breeze off the ocean. She saw a lady walking her dog, and as soon as the woman drew within hearing distance, Suzanne smiled and said to her, "Did your dog enjoy its spa treatments today?" The woman looked at her as if she were crazy. "How did you know my dog was just in the spa?" she asked. Suzanne immediately replied, "Because she told me so!"

Now that requires some unique attunement! However, for us humans, it is a very powerful and frequently overlooked or neglected "channel" of information. We are just now beginning to learn how much can be gleaned from the amazing animal beings who walk, fly, or swim in our midst and who share this earthly experience with us. No doubt, many esoteric schools are dedicated to translating the communications of our dear friends the whales, the dolphins, the bees, the llamas, the horses, and other four-legged creatures.

Although I am just learning to receive direct information from animals like my friend Suzanne, I am always thrilled to be with more advanced animal whisperers who can translate the thoughts of our wily creatures. I still remember a wonderful "reading" years ago by an animal communicator, who made contact with a sweet cat named Bob who happened to be living on a llama farm. Surrounded by other animals, he visited the donkeys and sheep (but always managed to evade the nearby coyotes). The llamas considered him part of their herd. One day while meditators were seated in a circle in the living room, this animal psychic must have asked Bob a question because she later confided that he felt he was the smartest creature in that whole room. (And he added that he was also the most handsome!)

I am grateful to Suzanne for opening up this area of pursuit; I don't know why it didn't occur to me before. If you are interested in learning more about Suzanne's way of channeling and her Co-Creative abilities both as a medium and healer, consult her website, c/o www.suzannedewees.com; you can also find her in Chapter 3 of my former work, *Channeling the Sacred*, published by GracePoint Publishing in 2020. In that book she shared about how her work has developed as a medium for deceased relatives and others who've passed on as well as that of a general channel connected with Light Beings in Light.

INFORMED BY A CROW

Taking Suzanne's guidance to heart, I sat and watched as crows gathered in the tree outside my window. Such amazing, sleek, ubiquitous creatures! Their intelligence and their mischief have always enchanted me. I remember hearing from Thoth in a channeled session with Danielle some time ago that crows, in fact, were Guardians of the *Akashic Records*. Now, that itself was hard to wrap my mind around. How could a bird that small carry that big a knowledge from the Universe? We learned about that because a crow had landed outside my friend Ann's window and remained there during the entire transmission. During the call, Ann was the one who shared about his presence with Thoth. And that's how we learned about the Crow's exalted status.

So I checked in with my dear friend the Crow, who happened to be perched outside my window. "Is this true?" I asked. Are you in fact keepers of such *records*?

Of course, it is true, you silly girl. Then he went on to *straighten* me out in terms of what I knew about crows. We are the known sentinels of the Universe, he said. We guard history; we guard the past, present, and future in terms of all collected knowledge. Do you think the simple 'Caw, caw,' you hear from us up in the trees is just us calling out for food or exchanging news of the weather? Don't be ridiculous. We have inborn sensors to warn us about food or predators. Of course, here where we live, our only predators turn out to be your automobiles—those big, clanking tin cans traveling down the road.

No, we've got pretty carefree lives, for the most part. If you hear our calls, it's most likely a sign that we're partying up here in the trees. You have no idea what a delight it is for us to be airborne. Flying brings the greatest pleasure. So does our constant treasure hunt for knowledge. Of course, we must tend to food gathering and caring for our young, but for the most part that involves easy scavenging; we don't have to line up in supermarkets, drug stores, or clothing outlets in order to take care of our basic needs.

You mistake our size and simple life and imagine us to be retro or mere simpletons. But you have no idea how cunning we really are—or how smart! You would be too if you turned out to be a sentinel for all knowledge. You humans have plotted out incredible charts of what you imagine is your evolutionary path. (Please pardon this summary, dear apes, monkeys, and other creatures! We find it very *animalist*—the only word that can summarize human prejudice in the same vein as the words *sexist* or *racist*. However, in those *evolutionary* charts you've lined everyone up as emerging from the ocean—first fish appear then frogs then other species, and then apes line up (who can barely stand upright), before the grand appearance of *homo erectus* and *homo sapiens*! And that's it! If you must know, it is not only an archaic and outdated rendering, but it's founded on a thoroughly inaccurate understanding of evolution. A lot of times what you mistake for "cawing" is just us up in the trees, laughing hysterically at the arrogance and foolishness of humanity.

Now consider the fact that you have much bigger brains than we do. You certainly pride yourself on that *gray* matter! But ponder deeply—

in the long run how well has that served you? Although you may refer to us as birdbrains, you don't see any of us contemplating nuclear war or beating up on our children. Although we may have an inborn pecking order, it would be very unlikely for us to carry out full-scale destruction. It is only that bald-headed earthbound creature named Alfred Hitchcock who'd ever dream up the idea of a flock of birds wishing to pounce or peck at humans. We have no interest in that.

In fact, if you knew us better, you would grasp how we actually work together as a collective. It's so much easier to get things accomplished that way. Did I mention that we even cooperate with *squirrels* if we're lining up for food at one of your bird feeders? Your scientists have remarked upon the fact that we actually contrive to use tools with our beaks and our feet; however, we would never in a million years construct a tool such as a gun, even if it put us at an advantage over other species. No, we're a hardy and long-lived species who love what we do, love all others, whether walking, swimming, or flying around in this environment. Most of all, we love carrying out our complex mission in multiple dimensions you may never have heard of.

If you think of us as small and stupid—we certainly won't try to disabuse you of that notion. But consider this—in all the years we've survived together on this particular planet, you've never managed to bring us down! Most of the time you don't even know we're here—listening, observing, taking notes, or commenting on things that eventually wind up in the *Akashic Records*. Though you tend to kill things off that are in any way different from you, we've never heard you call out, "Honey, it's time to eat! We're having roasted Crow-meat, and you know that's your favorite!"

CLEO SHARED THIS WHILE HER OWNER WAS SLEEPING

Now Cleo is a most unusual cat. A very Zen creature, Cleo shares a house with Annie, a cat who often tries to pick fights with her, leading their owner to keep them on separate floors. Cleo not only remains calm and unflustered through most ordeals but also helps out in a most unusual way. Ever since I began offering online Healing Touch to her owner, Cleo voiced her willingness to participate as an aid and avid co-worker.

It is truly amazing. First, I set up the Zoom session, and in just a few brief minutes my sweet client shows up, blanket at the ready with her laptop positioned in such a way that I can actually see her while she's lying supine on her couch. However, I pause before starting because once our owner is comfortably settled in, Cleo jumps up, acknowledging that all is well and that it's time for us to begin. It's uncanny the way she gazes at me on the screen before taking her position.

Generally she moves around on her owner's belly, sometimes kneading a particular spot, sometimes moving closer to her head or more towards her feet. Finally turning to face her owner, Cleo then finds a spot and reclines gracefully on her stomach. Again, she looks at the screen, as if signaling me to begin. While I do my assessment of her owner's energy field, Cleo pays rapt attention. Once I begin the actual work of transmitting Healing Touch, I receive definite feedback and commentary from her.

"You left off the upper body too soon. Can't you tell she still has some imbalance around her ears?" Little meows or pointing her whiskers in a certain direction underlines her point. So I go back to head and neck again, and sure enough there is a certain amount of heat needing to be dissipated as well as some slight congestion over the forehead. If the healing work is proceeding well, Cleo usually puts her head down and drifts off into her own reverie. If, on the other hand, there's too much indecision, again she turns to look at me directly on the screen. I can hear her saying, "Chill," or "Slow down," or sometimes in a more generous frame of mind, "This is exquisite! Keep up the good work."

Just the other day, when finishing up another session with Cleo's owner, I received a remarkable transmission from Cleo. She was unusually quiet this time around. So I asked her why she had remained asleep through most of the healing time (really, I was wondering without saying it—why had she stopped badgering me?). Then she spoke clearly and without faltering. Cleo told me that she was just testing my patience to see how well I could remain attuned to her owner, even if she interrupted or distracted me. So she had engaged in these different ploys. But finally she saw no need to continue with that process and added that my attunement was *adequate*. She also affirmed that the energy of healing was coming through purely and perfectly. In fact, she could now just settle down and receive healing as well. Because, once she realized that she had a crick in her neck that would not go away, she knew that it was only Healing Touch that would help her get back into balance.

RUMI HAS THESE OBSERVATIONS

Rumi is a precious white puppy living with his family not far from here in Alford. His family consists of mother, father, plus an empty nest, which often gets filled with three visiting adult children. Plus of course he has his other canine friend, Milo. Rumi laments the empty nest a great deal, for it has given him a sense of belonging and satisfaction to have many cheerful human friends around (not that Mom and Pop are not cheerful—on the contrary they're both incredibly fun and friendly). But Rumi is evidently the *runt* of this big litter, and he feels that the more the merrier always applies, and gives him a sense of safety—whether those present are human or canine.

Rumi has spent a lot of time getting to know Milo, his aging canine mentor, beautifully white with dark eyes covered by the presence of milky cataracts. Milo has hung on for a long time because he loves this family so much, but it's very clear that his doggy body can no longer hold up even in this kind and gentle environment. He can hardly walk to the kitchen to his feeding bowl, let alone go outside when Nature calls.

All of this is very puzzling to Rumi, who's taken lessons on everything from appropriate pet behavior with humans (especially learning not to jump on visitors), how to *smell* what's afoot in terms of energy and emotions, and how to contain his extraordinary *joie de vivre*, although clearly he does not excel in the latter category. Yet, he's well aware of the sacred mission entrusted to all dogs living with humans—and that is to be great friends, mentors, and guides.

Rumi clearly lets me know that his job is to attend to the energy and vibration of his owner's household. He moves around barking, prancing, or sitting by the door, always in an effort to re-balance whatever he senses is the predominant energy pattern. Most of the time his job is very easy, since his is a household where love abides. However, with Milo's failing physical health, Rumi's noticed a great deal of grief and sadness present in the environment that was never there before. In fact, he's never met up with these kinds of emotions in his very young life, and it's a little unsettling to him. He sometimes pines or stares at the door to the bedroom, if his owners are inside meditating. Although they're training him not to scratch on the door, it's one area of behavior he finds very difficult to accept.

Mostly, he's content to run and greet Mom or jump at Dad's ankles in a playful gesture. His message is always the same. Basically, he's thanking them for such a great life—for this wonderful place that has woods to roam in and streams outside. Inside the house, there are beautiful carpets alongside wooden floors that he loves because he can feel his paws clicking upon them as he runs from room to room. And best of all, his parents are now allowing him to enter their sacred room when they have positioned themselves to sit very still and commune in silence. He has learned that their word for such activity is *meditation*—but he's surprised they have to sit to achieve their goal. He knows that he's in that state in each and every moment, all the time, no matter what he's doing. And he's confident that eventually, as their good feelings return, that he will be accepted as the Household Guide (with Milo gone). For truthfully, no one's really told him he must contain his enthusiasm. They love him as he is, and his love for them in turn is boundless.

EVEN THE TREES SPEAK

Finding my way to the board walk that winds through Parson's Marsh in Lenox, I was amazed at the tumble-down nature of the woods that abutted the marshlands, which in turn faced out onto pristine waters.

"You are surprised to see us in this sorry state?" one of the trees asked me. I touched the birch tree whose yellowing bark was peeling off in multiple layers as if they'd stood too long out in the sun.

Some leafless Red maples then chimed in, "Look around you. Can you imagine this? Trees have fallen down everywhere. Old spruce, oak, ash, ancient walnut, fir trees, coniferous, deciduous—you name it—they're all piled up here, lying down, uprooted, or hanging on by only one frail limb."

It was the tallest of the white pines surveying everything, however, which informed me that I had inadvertently wandered into a "Tree Cemetery": "Can you imagine that they'd just leave us here to rot? Or to remain like that poor pine that bisected the old oak, hanging down the middle of his trunk?"

I looked to see what he was referring to and was amazed at how the trees seem to be holding each other up (or else weighing them down to the point of crumbling). But he had more to tell me.

"That poor pine fell the night of that horrid wind storm some weeks ago. The winds easily clipped along at 50 or 60 miles an hour; he didn't have a chance." Then the Tall Pine pointed me to a Red Maple who'd also fallen but her root system, framed in hardened mud and ferns easily stood five feet off the ground, like some dark table someone had hurriedly overturned. The roots stuck out like huge veins gnarled and twisted all along the table's grasping *hands*.

"Still, it's quiet here," murmured a small Ash. "You see squirrels, blackbirds, geese, and some random bird watchers here and there, but mostly we trees have the land to ourselves and we converse and share memories."

"Yes, that's true," replied the Tall Pine, "That is, among those of us who're still alive."

But the Ash kept on with the forest tour. "You see all those logs split apart with tufts of grass growing out of their limbs?" I nodded. "They were felled early on; no one dared move them, and this marsh became their graveyard."

"But we never mourn their passing," the Pine added. "For we trees stretch back hundreds of years and often have hundreds more years to go before we're done. Life is a complex but very slow-moving affair, punctuated by rain, thunder storms, wind, warm breezes, birds nesting on our branches, and the occasional passersby, such as yourself, pausing to gaze at us. Yet all we do is witness. And commune, and as Ash mentioned, we share memories that for us may stretch all the way back to the beginning of time."

"Wow," I thought to myself. "What a hard life." But old Pine caught me in the act, interrupting my thoughts. "Not nearly as hard as for you humans. You come and go quickly. But we carry on. We knew your parents and grandparents and maybe even the very first settlers here in Massachusetts. Since we never know when the next windstorm is going to dismember us, we sink our roots deeper and deeper into the Earth, delighted to have forged such a solid partnership through time. Sinking our roots provides a singular communion with all life forms while helping us remain firmly planted, drinking the soil's elixir, shading you, and meanwhile feeding our love right back to the sun, the sky, and the Earth beneath our roots."

This was almost too much to bear, and I wiped tears from my eyes. "You're part of our memories, now, dear One," I heard the Old Pine murmur as I slowly headed from the boardwalk to the pathway leading back to my car.

SWAN MEDICINE

"If only you humans knew how to help one another," a White Swan told me while she swam with her partner across the lake. I was puzzled by this non sequitur.

"Why do you say that?" I asked her.

"Because you continue making so much trouble for each other; it amazes us. If you were to study our posture or our progress, what do you imagine is the dominant theme?" she asked.

Moving into a more quiet, mindful state, the first thought that popped into my head was of course, peace.

"Exactly. It's peace we offer each other, and it's peace that we live in, moving in and out of the water, flying, or seeking a nice warm mound in the sun where we can sleep."

"Yes, but your lives, your whole mission and consciousness are different from us humans," I mused out loud.

"That's true," she replied. "However, you could learn more from us than we could from you."

"I'm not arguing that point," I replied.

"We bring you music, we bring you beauty, and we bring you peace. Just look at that sweet White Swan who left the water to go sit at the edge. She practically has her beak and her body blanketing that poor Black Swan over there."

"What's wrong with him?" I asked.

"Nothing's wrong, really. He just hasn't taken fully to the water yet. And he's sad because he recently lost his mate."

"Oh, so she's sheltering him," I said.

"Yes, sheltering and much more. She's breathing life into him. She's sending him energy particles that come from her breath and the sun."

"Wow! That's amazing."

"Yes, it is. Look now, he's getting up…"

And as I watched in sheer amazement, he had sloughed off his ennui and was heading rapidly after her in the water.

"Energy particles, indeed," I thought. We really do need to study Swan medicine.

A METAPHOR FOR SUFFERING

My friend Suzanne always has wise words for me, particularly during difficult times. I was going through a conflict with a close friend and wasn't sure if we'd be able to make it through and keep our relationship intact. During a particularly difficult stretch, Suzanne called and I was grateful to her once again for bringing me good tidings from the Animal kingdom.

"Think about this," she said. "Consider how monkeys carry their young through the jungle. Those baby monkeys have to hang on for dear life, clutching mama's fur, or anything they can get their hands on. After a while, they get quite adept at clinging, as they're flying through the air, but it can be nerve-wracking." I agreed with her as I could picture this unfolding.

"Now consider your feline species," she added. "Big cats, house cats—any kind of cats: think about how they carry their young." "It's by the scruff of their necks," I said. "You're right," Suzanne added— "By the scruff of their necks. So in order to be moved about, those kittens adapt to that hold by going limp. There's no fight—no resistance."

"Isn't that a great metaphor for suffering?" Suzanne then added. "We have to give up the fight!" I had to think about it for a few minutes. "You mean I can either hang on for dear life, clinging to these bizarre swings from *tree to tree*—or I can surrender, go limp, and just let myself be carried to the next place?

"Exactly," Suzanne replied.

"But I'm not sure that I want to be carried around by the scruff of my neck," I told her, and she laughed at the joke. "Of course you don't. But then think about all the ways you clutch or hold on tightly, fearing for your life!"

That too made sense. I pondered further and realized that no matter what seems to be happening or how upside down my life is, that I need to have faith in the process; it's leading somewhere, even if I can't see where because I'm caught in some Dark Night of the Soul. Then I realized that no matter what, Spirit has always carried me through to safety. The light at the end of the tunnel invariably shows up when it's least expected.

CHESTNUT MARE

Winding my way back home after work one evening, I stopped to gaze at the array of beautiful animals on the horse farm. From across the meadow, a chestnut mare saw me watching her. "God, you're so tall," I thought to myself.

"Of course I'm tall," she replied. "I'm a horse, after all."

"Yes, but horses come in all sizes!"

"That may be true," she replied, "But here at our riding academy we don't go in for midgets. We don't even have ponies among us."

"Do you like riding people around in circles?" I asked her, taking a look at the broad riding circle that was set off with wooden posts.

"Bah—that's for newcomers," she said. "Me, I'm lucky to canter out to the meadow, then head down to the woods, and finally stop for a brief drink in that stream that meanders through the valley."

Suddenly she stopped, put her head down as if foraging for worms, insects, or some small bit of tack in the dirt she sifted through. When her rider nudged her further along, she lifted her head and called out to me, "She's always in a hurry—see? She has no eye or ear for exploring and no nose for the roots or earthy treats along the ground."

I saw that her rider was impatient and kept kneeing her to get started toward the trail. But the mare was having none of that. She continued talking, "You should know that we're used to this, dear one. We've been carrying you now for hundreds of years. It's quite a business—this carrying people around. At first it felt really weird and uncomfortable; I tried to throw my first human. Then by degrees it became more manageable. But just imagine if you had to carry someone on your back all day. Of course, you no longer walk on all fours, but then think about it. You've seen dads carrying toddlers on their shoulders. Think what a strain it would be if they had to do that all day long."

I agreed what a hardship it would be and then began feeling the tug in my very own neck and shoulders.

"Of course, you don't require us all to be conveyors and carriers. But you have your different sports. Throughout time you've had us chasing foxes or racing neck-in-neck with our own kind, or even jumping over fences to prove our worth."

Slowly, I began seeing things in a different light. "But you've always gone along with the program?" I asked.

"Some do; some don't," she replied. "But the truth is that we'd rather be on the move. We were built to run. We'd rather be doing pretty much of anything you train us to do or entice us with your pretty words and fine treats and gestures. Anything that keeps us active winds up being a reasonable request."

And then the Chestnut Beauty added for emphasis: "Anything, that is, that keeps us from winding up in the glue factory."

TWO FISH YIELD UNEXPECTED SECRETS

This is George and I'll speak to you briefly, but quite honestly, I'm afraid I don't have much to say right now. Sitting here in the midst of all this human traffic, I confess that the lack of stillness and privacy serves as a great distraction.

Hello, I'm Georgiana and I'm circling around, keeping a lookout on my husband George, who no longer participates and who seems to be greatly troubled by our Piscean Kingdom.

George: I'm not *troubled*; that's not a good characterization. I'm simply complete. As in done. Over. Finished. I've had enough of roaming around this small space, which offers only a few caverns, rocks, and trees and maybe a tiny cave in which to sleep or continue one's explorations. Life here in this enclave no longer interests me; I've told you that before. Please don't take it personally.

Georgiana: I don't take it personally. Of course I too feel a sense of alienation; after all, our kids are still caught up in the fish race, playing hide and seek, exploring all there is to be explored. But I'm not yet done. There's still more to see and do and much more to learn. I'm perfectly content with the role of *Watcher*, which was assigned to me before you came on the scene.

George: Watcher is such a stupid role. What is there to watch in this 3x5 space? You've been through every nook and cranny; you've seen fish come and go, and you've raised our own brood in a matter of five or ten minutes. Don't you see? There's so much more to life than what we have here.

Georgiana: I understand that. I can see out the window just like you can. The difference is that I'm still embodied and I'm still right here, observing everything from a place of neutrality. For me, that provides a greater challenge and at the same time an even greater reward.

George: Well, I know nothing about that, having never been designated a *Watcher*. But it seems to me that I do a helluva lot more watching than you do.

Georgiana: That may be true, since you spend most of your time at the top of the tank, with your head touching the ceiling. What are you looking at with so much longing and anticipation?

George: I'm longing to get out of here. Look at that vast world surrounding us. Look at the people coming and going, as well as the young children who stop to gaze at us and follow our movements. Doesn't that excite you? Don't you want to be out there moving around in that larger world?

Georgiana: Not really. I'm content to be where I am. There's enough going on outside of me (and plenty to confront inside of me) to keep me busy and occupied here. It just makes me sad to see you floating up there for hours. Life has otherwise lost all its charm for you.

George: You're right on that score.

Georgiana: And the other thing that troubles me is that you no longer fulfill your promise. You've relinquished your Sacred Mission while you spend all that time looking outward.

George: Oh, I don't know about that. This older woman who's been staring at me for the last twenty minutes while she waits for her appointment with her doctor has certainly reaped the benefits of that time with me.

Georgiana: How do you know?

George: Can't you tell? My solitary placement here at the top of our tank has got her entranced. She may be watching me, but I've been keeping track of her just the same. In fact, I've been counting carefully. Her blood pressure has already dropped twenty points and is still plummeting. She won't need a higher dose of her medication when she sees the doctor.

Georgiana: Good work, George. That's fabulous!

George: Thank you. I knew you'd appreciate it.

ABOUT THIS MONKEY BUSINESS

Poor fish! To tell you the truth, we monkeys are a bit miffed. We thought you were going to pass us by completely. And it irks us that you seem to favor domesticated animals over those of us who run wild. While we feel sorry for those fish enclosed in that god-awful tank, we're not going to spend time dwelling on that. You see, as monkeys we need our freedom. We thrive on freedom. We depend upon these tree branches and bushes, the warm winds and the prevalence of fruits and blossoms, along with the pristine waters of our sacred environment. And we like that song someone wrote a long time ago, "Don't fence me in!"

Now your friend Suzanne didn't really understand about our young, when she compared us to the feline species. You see we move so quickly and adeptly through forest and jungle that our babies learn to cling to us—that much is true. But what you need to understand is that by the very nature of that movement, our young learn to navigate on their own. They pick up the speed and the efficiency through our means of travel; it gets embedded in the very cells of their body, and they become natural *movers and shakers*, able to move out on their own quickly. There's none of this angst or clinging for dear life. You humans really don't get us, do you?

Although we certainly don't mind when you dress up us monkeys and make us work with organ grinders or clowns, begging coins from customers; however, we get concerned when you miss out on our great Monkey Medicine. For we are one of the happiest and most creative tribes of animals on Earth! Of course, it's true that we don't have such lofty pretensions as the crows do in guarding knowledge for all time. But you don't realize something important—and that is, long ago we instructed those very crows in the art of play. We taught them around the globe in large webinars. No, sorry—correction. We taught *spiders* in webinars. We taught crows in Cro-hm format. Incidentally, speaking of spiders—did you know that after we had finished their training, that they changed the very nature of the way the spun their webs?

But let's get back to the crows. We gathered up hundreds and hundreds of crows over time and essentially taught them how to play. They were at first puffed up about their knowledge abilities and also lorded over us because they could fly. But soon the tables turned. You should have heard them laughing when we showed them how to roll down hills or jump over one another.

And then eons ago something important came about. The crows were able to combine play with knowledge in the *Akashic Records!* They grasped what we have instinctively known through the centuries—

and that is that play is one of the highest forms of wisdom. We're happy that they finally picked up on that.

And then of course, we continued fooling around with you humans. Where do you think that the idea of the 100th monkey came from? We had set up a vigil and signaled to monkeys from Jamaica to Africa to India and back again; in that very same instant all of us began washing potatoes. Luckily, your scientists got wind of this and advertised the maneuver as evidence of our great evolutionary powers and intra-species communication. But after all was said and done, we were just pulling your leg. You see, most of us don't really go in for raw potatoes and would much rather eat fruit. However, there's clearly no need to go out and wash bananas.

So we love this monkeying around business. If you had been with us in the beginning of time—or what's often called, *Creation*—you would have seen how important it was for us to monkey around with everyone's projects. We turned mountains into molehills. We helped reverse the tides. For a while, we even toyed with placing the firmaments in reverse order—but it didn't work out because the oceans kept pouring downward, filling up the sky below. On other planets without gravity, however, that adjustment worked perfectly well.

So you see, your opening Creation story was wrong! We were in fact present at Creation and came up with many useful ideas. We even managed to sneak four of our children onto Noah's Ark (against code), so later on it turned out that we had greater numbers as a species than your cows or horses. But of course you can see that we're playing with you again, and if you must know, that's been our assignment all along. We'd have to give humanity a "5" out of a possible "10" in terms of learning to frolic and play; goats, of course, are right up there at "10," as are puppy dogs, parrots, dolphins, otters, moles, and magpies. It's taken us a long time to train every species, and we almost gave up on house cats.

But we're always thrilled to return to our own haunts and bask in the mere beauty and absurdity of existence. As a matter of fact, one hundred years ago we inspired certain of your Dada playwrights and artists to put together what you call, the *Theater of the Absurd.* But look how many centuries it took for you to come up with that, and all along you thought it was your original idea! It was hard enough for us to adapt when you started repeating "Not my monkey" all the time and then later on added, "It's not my circus." Well, we beg to differ.

In fact, dear ones, we monkeys are happy to announce that we're still working with you. And we continue training you in small pods or groups that join us on several playing fields. In addition, due to changes in the atmosphere, we are available for appointments on Zoom or FaceTime, although quite honestly, we'd rather help you play with Creation right in your own home! It *is* your circus—trust us. Or better yet—come join us in *our* home—the mad habitat where creatures play for no particular reason at all. Remember, though. There *is* a method to our madness. For it's mainly in playing that you discover the true *emphasis* of Creation. We hope you join us!

Part Three:

Jumping to Conclusions

OUR INVITATION TO YOU

This is Thoth and the Council of Light coming forward to complete this process of Divine Co-Creation with you—our dear earthly counterparts. We're happy you've had time to visit with our friends from the Animal kingdom, who track right along with us and continually contribute their magic to our Creation. Communicating with different species in many ways is like moving back and forth or in and out of different lifetimes (all within this lifetime), by learning how to be the Connector of Consciousness of all sentient Beings. Thich Nhat Hanh, a wonderful champion of Mindfulness, talked at length about the nature of Inter-Being. That's where you go to make connections. (8)

The implication is that there is a place existing *between* Beings, no matter what species you are, that is available for making contact, if you are sensitive to its presence. In fact, many Light Beings who're known as Animal communicators have developed that awareness and are sensitive to messages from different creatures that are trying to communicate with you. It's a beautiful alliance, and in a certain way, it allows you to bring the sweetness of *heaven and earth* together in one contiguous experience.

But now we're hoping to move on, since our conversation is gradually coming to completion. Still, we have a few thoughts we want to leave with you. Once again, take a deep breath. Although we may be leaving this work, we are by no means leaving y*ou*. Isn't it clear that all that's been presented here has been created on your behalf? With what we've been pouring forth, it must be obvious! This invitation is extended to you in the hopes that you are ready to engage freely in Co-Creating with the Divine!

At this point, we wish to make it *official*, so we are inviting you to take up your calling in earnest, and we'd like to say with *Godspeed*— since we're now conjoined in such a holy undertaking together. As you prepare to take up this work even more deeply and profoundly, we invite you to step up to the plate in the fullness of who you are—and we do mean *fullness*. For you often step forward two or three steps and then move back five, or you try to move to the back or even sidle out of the "room" altogether. Your excuse is that there are too many unsuitable parts of you, which by their nature make you *ineligible* for the cause. You can drop that theory now. Let it go.

We return to this theme again and again because in your Old Paradigm view of things, there are still vestiges of higher or lower than and better or worse. Jo Ann frequently excludes herself when she feels impatient or has angry outbursts. However, her greatest and most cunning means of self-exclusion is to indulge in the illusion that she's forever unloved. It's such an easy card to pull from the deck—from anyone's deck. But in her case because she lives alone and doesn't always hear from her family or friends—that makes it even more preferable as her specific card to play.

It definitely takes some getting used to—and that is this notion that *all parts* of you are wanted! And it's not just your heavenly-smilingly-sweet-Pollyanna personality. In deference to gender equality, by the way, we will now shift that term to include a Sheldon-so-happily-Harry kind of being.

You see, you vibrate along a very broad spectrum of frequencies—much wider and farther along that you can imagine or have even perceived based on your earthly *vision*—or your attunement to earthly *sound*. We know how much you abhor the lower, slower vibrations—we hear from you frequently on that score. They seem to envelop you in sloth, torpor, anger, fear, or envy. What a nice job your Ten Commandments have done in helping you discard or despise that particular end of the spectrum! In fact, it's interesting for us to note that out of all ten pieces of guidance, only a few gave you any hint about good living—in terms of experiencing joy and heightened awareness, or appreciation for the abundance and love in your life! The best you could do was to honor your parents and try to keep the Sabbath. Think about it!

But we're getting a little off point here. What we'll reiterate time and again is this need for you to step up to the plate with all parts of you *intact*—from the lowest (or most detestable) to the highest (or most sacrosanct). For, you see, everything eventually steps out of its form—out of its physical or emotional expression and essentially returns to its original state, which simply translates as pure unadulterated energy. Energy is always in motion. Even in this moment your energy is reconfiguring itself—changing and moving in new directions. You sing "Do re mi," but its notes can take you out of the so-called *Solfeggio* scale (9) and introduce you instead to sounds you've never heard or could ever contain at this level of consciousness.

So too, you have many unknown parts of the *scale* within you. Although you may dislike the aspects that seem to vibrate in a low G or even lower C, still your voice cracks when you try to go two or three octaves higher. And how many singers are there in your world who can actually sing more than four octaves? (Not many, let us inform you...)

Even within your physical body, you vibrate at different frequencies. Your fingers and your toes have their own vibratory pattern, different from that of your lungs or your kidneys. Among all your organ systems, your heart has the highest frequency of all—yes, even higher than the brain, despite what certain nerds might insist on believing! And yet you don't despise your fingers or your toes for vibrating in a lower register than your brain or your heart! You would not consider it mandatory to cut off two or three toes or two or three fingers in order to qualify for the higher vibrations necessary to enter the heavenly realms—i.e. into Co-Creation with the Divine?

That theory sounds ridiculous, of course, but it does relate to how you might reject certain parts of your character that you consider inferior. And that leads to further guilt, anger, or denial. Of course, the church invented confession to get around that obstacle, but somehow that has not fully released your guilt or shame because you have to keep going back every Sunday to provide more *grist* for the evangelical *mill*. Some religions have pared confession down to once a month—some have you only going back once a year. Either way, it's not the brightest solution for getting your priests and rabbis remunerated.

Of course, we're playing here. Although we may be taking this point too far, we are trying to paint the picture in a number of different ways to help you understand that there is no longer a need for you to divide yourself into parts. You love talking about the Light and the Shadow. The Righteous and the Sinful. Or when the Good and Bad turned into Ugly. Now we're not talking about behavior in this context nor are we condoning anything outside of the Realm of Love. Quite the contrary; in fact, our task is to remind you again and again until at last you land fully with us in the Realm of Oneness. We exist in this together—all parts, all aspects, and all vibrations— within the broad spectrum and the profoundly wide and ample state of Love. Jo Ann is remembering a hymn she's heard quite a few times, "There is a Wideness in God's Mercy" that comes to mind on this occasion. And you have no idea how far or how wide we can go.

Not only that, when you step up to join us, you grasp how in fact all parts of you are not only accepted but also are *needed* to join in. You need all your toes to provide stability and balance. You need all your fingers to point and grasp and hold and write and knead and touch—all the lovely things that hands and fingers do as a cooperative gesture. It's not just your hearts we've enlisted to join with us—it's every part of your being—including the physical, the subtle, and the Divine.

Though we may speak with urgency, we are in no way impatient. We know the Divine order of things; we know that with every step, your consciousness is evolving, growing, and expanding beyond its outworn boundaries into realms and spaces inconceivable for you to have inhabited before. But you are now. Whoever termed the phrase *bandwidth* had no idea how far that term would stretch or what it might include about your creation that could enlarge and extend its reach. Remember Jabez's prayer? (10) He asked to have his "territory" enlarged. Little did he know what he was getting himself into, but we're happy to relate that he's still on it and he's still growing his territory. So it's good for you to realize that this expansive effort of Co-Creation will take you into realms and universes you had no idea existed. And it will extend your reach beyond the known worlds of your habitation.

Some time ago, my dear brother Yeshua spoke to you about the difference between inclusion and exclusion. It takes a broad leap of faith to jump into inclusion. In so many lifetimes you've been told you're not good enough or smart enough or rich enough or righteous enough to be accepted and included—wherever you are. Now you don't need a society, a school or a supervisor—nor does a pulpit or a partner need to tell you anything—you've managed to imbibe the perfect formula through lifetimes that helps you put yourself down in singular and specific ways!

So in our final moments, we wish to say, "Stop!" This will be the most short-term therapy you'll receive from us, and if need be, you can post a sign on your mirror or your door repeating the message:

Stop it! Of course, you're free to add more gentle words, such as, "Smile," or "Be the Light," or "Rejoice and be glad!"

Although we're joking again, in a way the underlying message remains the same. It is time to accept all parts of yourself as indivisible and acceptable in terms of the Oneness you share with Creation. Your animals tell you that it's so. Your golden retriever doesn't need you to qualify with a Phi Beta Kappa in order to jump up and slobber on your face. Your plants, your trees, the sun is shining repeatedly with warm greetings, and the stars all dazzle with the light of a thousand smiles saying, "Welcome!"

We echo that statement; in fact, we might add, "Welcome back!" We're delighted that you are here. We're so happy you allow that splendid light of yours to shine. We're so glad that you have all octaves of yourself blissfully present and currently engaged in this delightful project of Co-Creating with the Divine.

CREATING CEREMONY

Nowadays, few people grasp the reasoning behind or the need for creating ceremony before significant events that are about to unfold in their lives. Though various rituals still abound, needless to say, they've gotten a little tired and worn out. Weddings, bar and bat mitzvahs, or graduations become opportunities more to consume hors d'oeuvres and cocktails than to honor the person or the transition. Even the new brand of gender-reveal events for newborns is somewhat of a glorified mechanism for partying or dressing in the appropriate *colors*.

If you think about the nature of ceremony, it's principally designed to help you connect with Spirit and announce your new intention. If you're changing roles, relationships, moving into new territory, or bringing forth a great new work, then ceremony provides the launch pad and starting point. It functions as communication with the Divine. Besides invoking the Divine, however, ceremony is designed to help you *partner* with the Divine in order to achieve the highest and best outcome for all concerned.

So when you decide to create ceremony, let it be filled with magic and innovation, for in effect, ceremony that achieves its purpose always comes through in the language of Spirit. It's a process that gradually takes on a life of its own. Take time to get clear with your intention when you start out, and then weave that into the birthing of this bright new conception of yours. Let the ceremony speak to you on its own terms, directing you to perform in alignment with the kind of images that fulfill its calling in the best possible way. As you do so and as you gain heightened perception of the energies involved, you will sense and feel the manner in which the ceremony is actually welcoming in a whole new *era*—and with it a quantum field of new possibilities. Watch how it ushers in the ideal environment from which your creation can be birthed and brought forward. Then give thanks, for your ceremony has become the midwife guiding you into your new future.

A FOUR-PART CEREMONY OF CONNECTION

So let us begin. Light a candle. If you have sage or incense, let it waft through the room where you've chosen to do ceremony. It helps clear the energies and release any negative vibrations from your field, thereby inviting in the Divine. (Of course, be careful not to set off the fire alarm in the process.)

As we move toward completion, this is a perfect time to imagine the whole ritual, or what you might term the "Coming Out" ceremony on behalf of yourself and your new Creation. You may want to read through this entire section before settling into a specific part. However, everything that's included here is designed to help you arrive fully at the LAUNCH pad.

After establishing the sacred space in which your ceremony unfolds, find a comfortable place in which to sit, turn off all phones and devices, and give yourself this precious time in order to attune inwardly and become grounded. Before beginning, make sure you have a tablet, device, or paper nearby for writing during a later stage of this process.

Part One

Take a moment to withdraw into a calm, internalized state of meditation. Use your breath or any other techniques that work for you in heading back to center. This is a momentous and exciting time in terms of your Creation; however, in the beginning, you want to align with Source and be as closely connected to your work as you can be; therefore, starting out in meditation is a great way to *open the channels*. You may also engage some of the practices that we introduced in a prior chapter, such as humming, contemplative walking, and/or silent focused attention. After five or ten minutes, or however long you need to settle in fully, allow full waking consciousness to return as you gently come back up to the surface.

Part Two

The name of this section is "Calling Forth my Creation." Whether you have a work in progress—a book, a program, a work of art, a sculpture, a curriculum for learning, a meal plan, a move, a new business venture, or anything at all that you wish to call into form (at any stage of development along the *spectrum* of Creation), take a few moments to bring this work to mind. Do you remember the message that we provided about the Consciousness that's encoded in whatever you create, and how the action of creating bequeaths life and energy into what you bring forth? Now is the time to recognize the truth of that and to create a vivid encounter.

It may seem strange to consider your project as a living entity endowed with a consciousness just like yours; however, that is what happens when you bring things to *light*! So let this be a time of meeting up with whatever it is that is presently asking to come into form—it may even be overjoyed to be invited in and to claim its particular form of expression.

Before you begin writing, we're asking you to give this book or venture a *name*. If you already have a title, that's fine. But if you haven't thought one up, then it's fine to slide one in here just for the purposes of our meditation. You may call it, "My Dream Encounter with a New Business," or "The Meal You'll Remember Forever." Whatever it turns out to be, it's helpful to give it a name. You can always change it later on, as it grows its own *identity*.

Now, with your writing materials at hand, take out two "sheets" of paper or designate two pages on your computer or laptop. At the top of the first page, place the heading, "Dear Creation"—or whatever you choose to call it. That's all you need to write. At the bottom of that same page, sign it, "Love," and then write your first name. At the top of the second sheet, you'll reverse that process. At the top of the second sheet, simply write, "Dear," and then your first name. Drop all the way down to the bottom of the same page, and sign it with the name you've given your new work. So it might read something like, "Love, Your Blockbuster Book" or "Love, Your Joyful Journeys Travel Agency."

Then the writing that follows conforms to the way these two letters are set up on your pages. With the first one in hand, take a moment to actually connect with your Creation; then pour out all your thoughts, wishes, desires, fears, imaginings, and ideas in bringing together the elements that may be needed. By the way, this one page can lengthen into two or three or twelve or twenty, as needed. We just wanted to provide the format. When you've finished your first letter, sit back and take time to reflect on what you've written. Then picking up pen or returning to your keyboard, proceed to the second letter—which, this time will be addressed to you from the "Consciousness" of that new Creation.

Give it time. Thoughts will pour forth. As you sit in receptive mode, bordering on meditation, you may be surprised to find how much thoughtfulness is already encapsulated in that work and how many wonderful ideas pop up to the surface, once you allow space for reciprocal communication. It's not just that you're creating this work—this work *itself* is nudging you to guide it into its fullest expression imaginable. As a matter of fact, we could say that once you're both engaged, you're simultaneously *creating each other*!

So this is the format with which you carry out this communication. It doesn't have to end here, by the way; you can return, time and again, to download new "letters" or suggestions between you and your Creation about the best way to proceed with this work.

Part Three

Now return to your seated meditation. Take the next few minutes to absorb and integrate the information that has come through to you, or even to await a different *nudge* from the work itself. Before you begin the writing process, gathering up prayers, affirmations, and words of encouragement; however, take out a large piece of paper or some cardboard, and place the name of your Creation in a prominent place where you can see it. Or you can draw a picture or some other illustration of what it is. After all, it represents the Consciousness of this new work and has a place in this Ceremony right near you. Place the drawing, word, or representation where you can come back to it, gaze at it and remember all you've already perceived about your Creation.

Affirmations and Prayers

Now once again turn to your writing materials. Only this time you'll be writing specific prayers or affirmations that link you with your heart's desire as well as helping produce energy, light, and forward momentum welcoming in this Creation.

Depending on what's needed, you might affirm that you have everything you need in this moment to bring forth a work of clarity and excellence. Or you may wish to affirm that all the partners and Co-Creators you need are now showing up in the best possible way to promote this extraordinary event. Or you may pray for guidance and strength to give it your best shot! Or—and this might be fun to consider—you could sit with the Consciousness of your project and create affirmations in concert—things you know that you both want to bring forth together!

After you've written a number of prayers or affirmations that bring you into a space of joy and positivity, take a moment to reflect. Have you said everything you need to say in regard to this forthcoming work? Do your affirmations handle any leftover doubts or fears? Once you're convinced that your list is complete, the next task is to read each one out loud to yourself. Take your time with this; try reading in a style that mimics *Lectio Divina*, or the religious practice of reading slowly and thoughtfully to allow words to turn into prayer. Let the power of these affirmations penetrate your consciousness and bring you to a place of clarity and confidence. Your work is on its way! You may even choose to record these affirmations so you can listen to them again, but either way, you've done excellent work in fulfilling the important aspects of this ritual. Prepare now for the conclusion of your "Ceremonial Process."

Part Four

You have done all the groundwork to complete this *Ceremony* that fully welcomes your new Creation into form. This final part is divided into two parts: Read through entirely and then decide if you want to give greater focus to the ritual of fire or the ritual of repetition. Depending on your preference, you're free to engage with either or both as part of this conclusion.

Ritual of Repetition

First, read or recite the prayers out loud. Repeat certain affirmations that really resonate for you at this time. If you have musical ability, then imbue each line with a melody. Singing your affirmations allows them to *sink in* even more deeply! From a seated position, now shift into a lying down position on your bed or your sofa. Let these words continue to echo as you close your eyes and drift into a soft internalized focus, often referred to as *yoga nidra*, or yogic sleep. It's perfectly fine, by the way, if you happen to fall asleep. You will carry these words and sounds with you in their mantra-like form where they will resonate at the deepest layers of your being.

Ritual of Fire

For this part of the ritual, you can use candles, your fireplace, if you have one, or even a grill or wok you can safely use to burn things outdoors. On small sheets of paper, write down one or two things that may have been obstacles that you're now letting go of. On several other sheets of paper, write down the most inspirational messages about your new Creation (including any of the prayers or affirmations you've already written). Also include a few words about how this work is your great contribution to the world.

Acknowledging the presence of your Guides and helpers, light some candles near your Creation sheet to illuminate its presence and power. Next, stepping outside or into the kitchen, safely burn both sets of small papers. Watch them burn and let them go. Know that their messages have been received and fully accepted by Spirit, and so has your over-arching intent and your heart's desire.

Finally, sit with your new Creation, welcoming its presence fully into your life and allow it to welcome you into its life as well. End your Ceremony with any prayers, poems, or songs that inspire you and remind you of what an extraordinary *Creator Being* that you are!

AND FINALLY—TUNE IN!

Now look to your breathing pattern; return to stillness and bask in the aftermath of your ritual. What's happened during this interim? Has anything new occurred to you after doing this ceremonial activity? Just for the moment, though, sit back, rest, and allow everything to be integrated.

You'll find in short order that you've entered the Sacred Portals of *Creation-on-Demand* where amazing new ideas, combined with ingenious ways of mounting them as well as all kinds of inspiration are pouring in at top speed. Soon it will begin to dawn on you that have entered flow. You, the Work, and the Divine have now coalesced into a most beautiful experience of Co-Creation—and it is one that we can only describe as FLOW. Everything comes naturally. Everything arrives in perfect order. From here on in this work has taken on a life of its own and unfolds in a delightful and continuous flow.

Relax. Feel how easy it is to be in flow. Can you recognize the signs? Now, as you continue working, tune in. Listen to the music of the Spheres. It is beyond miraculous. No orchestra on Earth could possibly reproduce the magnificent tones or harmonies available out here in *Divinity*. And when we've combined our efforts together in these bold new Co-Creations, we promise you that the results will easily step out of known harmonic scales to reach unheard of Octaves of Pure Love and Delight.

So once again look around. Take in all the wonderful aspects of Creation—yours and everyone else's. Notice the quality of air and sunlight. Wherever you are, look out the window, or open the front door. Is wind present? Is there rain? How many dogs have you spoken to today? How many birds? And when you sat at your desk or puttered in the garage or in the kitchen, tell us who was puttering with you? Surely, they've been making enough noise to draw your attention, for even now we can see them jumping about in pure joy. You remember the facts of *real* Creation. So as we've mentioned on several occasions—it's time for you to acknowledge that your house is full of monkeys!

> With that, dear Light Beings,
> Know that we're also *jumping*!
> That is, we're jumping for joy with you—
> As your new Creations come through,
> For we celebrate all that you do.
>
> Our Love and prayers are with you.
> As are we!

Chapter Notes

Chapter 3:

1: *The Atma Gita* forms part of a collection of ancient Hindu scriptures whose origin is unknown but is attributed to teachings from Krishna to his beloved disciple Uddhava and is likely to have surfaced around 200 BCE, roughly the same time as the better-known scripture: *The Bhagavad Gita.*

Chapter 4:

2. *The Great Pretender* is a popular song recorded by the vocal group the Platters with Tony Williams on lead vocals. It was released in November 1955.

Chapter 9:

3. Bapuji (or dear father) was the affectionate name for Swami Kripalu, who visited the US from 1977-1981 and taught at the Pennsylvania ashram named after him. He was one of the greatest Kundalini masters of the 20th century in India and was also a classical musician, playwright and storyteller, who outlined the basic principles of *sahaj* or spontaneous yoga in his masterpiece: *The Science of Meditation.*

Chapter 11:

4. Quoted with Danielle Rama Hoffman's permission from recently channeled messages in March, 2021, from Thoth and the Council of Light: for more information, see the following section outlining Additional Resources, or consult: www.DivineTransmissions.com

Chapter 14:

5. *Transitions: Making Sense of Life's Changes.* By William Bridges, Published by Addison-Wesley Publishing Company, New York, 1980.

Chapter 18:

6. The poem "Outwitted" was published in *Shoes of Happiness and Other Poems*, by Edwin Markham, Doubleday, Page and Company, NY, 1921.

Chapter 22:

7. *Prayers from the Ark* was published in 1947. Originally in French, it was written by Carmen Bernos de Gasztold and translated into English by Rumer Godden.

Chapter 32:

8. Thich Nhat Hanh, as quoted in *How to Love (Mindfulness Essentials)*, Parallax Press, Berkeley, CA, 2015

9. **The *Solfeggio* Scale:**
In music, solfège, also called **solfeggio**, is a technique for teaching sight singing; each note of the score is sung to a special syllable, called a solfège syllable (or "sol-fa syllable"), as in Do re mi *sol fa.* The *Solfeggio frequencies* are a six-tone set of musical **tones**

that date back to ancient times. When sung in harmony, these **tones** were considered to be sacred and to confer blessings on those who listened to the music.

10. The Prayer of Jabez

"Oh that you would bless me indeed,

And enlarge my territory,

That your hand would be with me,

And that you would keep me from evil."

As quoted in *The Prayer of Jabez* by Bruce Wilkinson and David Kopp, Multnomah Publishers, Sisters, Oregon, 2000.

Additional Resources

For anyone who wants to dive into the full experience of Danielle Rama Hoffman's collected works channeling Thoth and the Council of Light, you can either log onto her website, listed below, or check for these works on Amazon:

The Temples of Light, by Danielle Rama Hoffman, Bear and Co. Press, VT, 2009

The Council of Light, by Danielle Rama Hoffman, Bear and Co. Press, VT, 2013

The Tablets of Light, by Danielle Rama Hoffman, Bear and Co. Press, VT, 2017

Danielle is an international coach and channel, keeper of the Ascended Master Lineage of Thoth, leader of the New Paradigm of Unity Consciousness and successful entrepreneur since the early '90s. In addition to her many programs, she also holds an imprint with GracePoint Publishing entitled *Scribes of Light*. If interested, you can learn about her programs, retreats, and high-level mentoring with Thoth on her website: www.DivineTransmissions.com

Jo Ann Levitt is available for private consultations, keynote talks, or personal retreats and workshops. If you'd like to follow up with any of the books mentioned by Jo Ann in this work or learn about her online services, please consult her website: www.joannlevitt.com or look for these on Amazon:

Channeling the Sacred: Activating Your Connection to Source, GracePoint Publishing in Collaboration with the imprint: Scribes of Light, Colorado Springs, CO, 2020

Prayers for the Pandemic, Xlibris, 2020

The Twenty-first Century Gospel of Jesus Christ, as told to Jo Ann Levitt, Xlibris, 2019

(Also in Spanish version): *El Evangelio de Jesucristo del Siglo Veintiuno*, Xlibris, 2020

The Pilgrim of Love, Monkfish Book Publishers, New York, 2004

Sibling Revelry: 8 Steps to Successful Adult Sibling Relationships, with her sister and brother Marjory & Joel Levitt, c/o Dell Publications, NY, 2001

GUIDED CEREMONY
OF WELCOME

Below is the script that can be used for a Ceremony or Ritual that you complete on your own:

It can be read out loud or used to accompany the actual recorded version, which is offered as a gift to you by the author.

If you've been following the details of our final rituals in *Co-Creating with the Divine,* I'd like to present you now with this guided journey to help you complete your process and to fully welcome in your NEW CREATION!

Before you settle in, first take a few minutes to establish your sacred space—your container for connecting with the Divine. Take a look around and decide what is needed to create the perfect context for welcoming your New Creation.

Whether you light candles, sage, or incense, be deliberate and focused in acknowledging this precious area where you have labored and are now about to give birth to your splendid new work. And then move into position where you feel warm and comfortable and can journey with comfort and ease.

As you land, sense that the space within and around you is opening a portal to the Divine. You may choose to lie down. Or you may simply sit and receive. Allow your breathing to slow down and your thoughts to withdraw inward. Feel your whole body relaxing, letting go of tension, and at the same time feeling drawn to the unfolding of this journey with its sacred joy and magic. In letting go, you are automatically carried forward. For we all journey, whether we're aware of it or not. Now is the time to move into ease and focused awareness as well as conscious collaboration, all of which allows for the joy of journeying with Spirit.

Breathe and relax. Now in your mind's eye, step out of your current surroundings and welcome yourself into the alternate world of the journey. Feel that you are entering a beautiful, serene, and vibrant place, perhaps in the mountains, on the beach, or in a space well known to you from prior travels. Take in the air, the gift of sunlight, and the power of mountains, trees, or water. As you move fully into this landscape, take a walk around, note the beauty and pristine quality of all that surrounds you. Receive the welcoming spirit of nature as you travel, and know that she is embodying what has now become your task as well. As you sit immersed in this sacred place, offer up any prayers of thanksgiving that may occur for you. Offer thanks for what you and the Divine have brought forth. And then with great anticipation, prepare to welcome your amazing new Creation right here, right now in this precious natural habitat.

Imagine that your work, which though it has been conscious all along, is now approaching you, *embodied* in its particular shape and form, and is coming to greet you and sit by your side. Take time to commune fully. Feel the presence of this work completed and having its own distinct Signature energy.

Once you have established contact, discuss with each other if anything more is needed in terms of this birthing process. What does this work ask of you? And what do you desire to receive from this Creation? This is the grand launching time; this is the mutual moment of welcome. You welcome your Creation into form; your Creation welcomes you as its champion.

As you sit in communion with each other, feel yourselves now being surrounded by the presence of many Guides and Light Beings in Spirit. All of them come forth to celebrate you as they join together in a broad circle, each one offering joy and appreciation for the consummation of this work. Now they gently circle you and your Creation. Notice how these Light Beings each have cups of shimmering liquid light that they are lifting up as an offering to you. It is a divine toast; drink this draft of celebration; enjoy—for you and your work are being gently launched into the universe. As you listen closely, you can hear music while Light Beings proclaim to you:

Listen to the music of the Spheres. It is beyond miraculous. No orchestra on Earth could possibly reproduce the magnificent tones or harmonies available here in the land of *Divinity*. Now that we've combined our efforts to bring forth your bold new Creation, we promise you that the results will easily step out of the known harmonic scales to reach unheard of Octaves of Pure Love and Delight. So rejoice with us!

Feel how your bright conception has been brought forth in light and in love. There is a great movement from which Light and Sound now pour forth, with brilliant colors matching the multiplicity of amazing sounds; you may be moved to sing or acknowledge this magic in any way that you desire. After a brief time, you can feel the Light Beings gently receding, and shortly after, your Creation nods to you in thanks, departing the Ceremony to go out and create its own brand-new environment. You can see it taking its place fully present, fully grounded, and fully acknowledged all throughout the multiple dimensions of reality.

And now in your own way, slowly take leave of the Ceremony as you return to the sacred space from which it emanated, breathing, resting, and allowing the work to be fully integrated within you. You can feel the glow of all that has transpired; although you've completed the journey, it remains with you as a subtle treasure from the Divine. Acknowledge yourself and acknowledge your Creation, for you are both complete.

The Author and her *Mentor* in Acapulco circa 1979

ABOUT THE AUTHOR

Longtime spiritual counselor and teacher, Jo Ann Levitt sheds new light on the practice of channeling as co-creation in her latest work: *Awakening to the Power of Source: Your Guide to Co-Creating with the Divine*. A prolific author as well as lecturer and program designer, Jo Ann was a senior Kripalu faculty member for thirty years and continues to teach meditation and provide spiritual counseling at Canyon Ranch in the Berkshires.

Through years of channeled writing and teaching, Jo Ann recognizes the need for each of us to partner with Spirit in order to bring forth works that are worthy of our deepest spiritual leanings and that serve the highest good. This Guide is the fifth book in a series of channeled works that also include: *Channeling the Sacred: Activating your Connection to Source*, as well as *The Twenty-First-Century Gospel of Jesus Christ,* along with its Spanish version, *El Evangelio de Jesucristo del Siglo Veintiuno*. In addition, Jo Ann wrote *Prayers for the Pandemic*—an anthology of prayers and poems about that difficult time period.

For more great books, please visit Scribes of Light Press online at:
https://gracepointpublishing.com/product-category/books-cards/
gracepointpublishing.com/product-category/scribes-of-light-press/

SCRIBES OF LIGHT
—— P R E S S ——

Made in the USA
Columbia, SC
26 August 2021